COLOURS
of Australia

THE QUILTERS' GUILD *gratefully acknowledges development assistance from:*

J.B. Fairfax Press Pty Limited, for their endorsement of this project; Kylie Winkworth, for her curatorial guidance; Dianne Finnegan (Showing the Colours), and Margaret Wright (Introducing the Colours of Australia) for their contributions as authors; Karen Fail (editor of the artists' statements); and to the other members of the organising subcommittee: Larraine Scouler (chairman), Megan Fisher, Narelle Grieve, Carolyn Sullivan and Isobel Lancashire.

Regional Tours coordination and management by:

The Arts Councils of New South Wales, Victoria, Queensland and Tasmania; South Australian Touring Exhibitions Program; Crafts Council of the Northern Territory, and Art On The Move, Western Australia.

For permission to reproduce text or patterns from their publications: The Road from Coorain, *Jill Kerr Conway (William Heinemenn Limited);* The Appliqué Workshop, *Cheryl Arnott (Penguin Books Australia Limited);* Machine Appliqué Made Easy, *Jan Brooke (National Book Distributors and Publishers).*

EDITORIAL
Managing Editor: Judy Poulos
Editorial Assistant: Ella Martin
Editorial Coordinator: Margaret Kelly
Photography: Andrew Payne
Illustrations: Lewis Chandler, Lesley Griffith

DESIGN AND PRODUCTION
Manager: Sheridan Carter
Senior Production Editor: Anna Maguire
Picture Editor: Kirsten Holmes
Design and Layout: Michele Withers

This edition first published in 1995 for
Quilters' Resource Inc.
P.O. Box 148850
Chicago, IL 60614

Published by J.B. Fairfax Press Pty Limited
80-82 McLachlan Ave
Rushcutters Bay, NSW 2011, Australia
A.C.N. 003 738 430

Printed by Toppan Printing Co, Hong Kong

JBFP 335

COLOURS OF AUSTRALIA
Directions in Quiltmaking
ISBN 0 9629056 1 5

COLOURS
of Australia

Directions in Quiltmaking

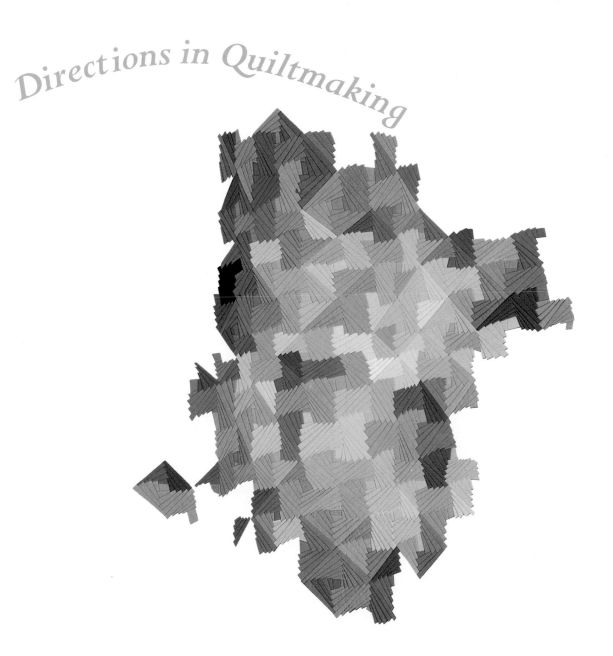

THE QUILTERS' GUILD
AUSTRALIA

Quilters' Resource Inc.

CONTENTS

In her monumental study The Crafts Movement in Australia: A History (1992, UNSW Press), Grace Cochrane describes the rapid expansion of all the arts and crafts in the 1970s, fuelled by the policy of the then prime minister Gough Whitlam of fostering the development of an Australian identity through the arts.

In this environment, humble domestic crafts were being reinterpreted as art, and quilts were gaining recognition. Many were content to follow received patterns; others produced quilts out of necessity, which were sometimes constructed out of old clothing and fabric samples. In general, those quilts were seen as an opportunity to create something of beauty for the home.

Acceptance of quilts as worthy of inclusion in art galleries has had a profound effect,

SHOWING THE COLOURS – PAST, PRESENT AND FUTURE

raising the status of quiltmaking to an art form, as well as raising public consciousness. Galleries that show quilts find their attendances increasing dramatically and, as a consequence, are staging more quilt exhibitions. In 1986, a seminal exhibition of Marjorie Coleman's quilts at the Fremantle Art Gallery, near Perth in Western Australia, attracted ten thousand visitors.

In 1985, Barbara Macey, Susan Denton, Jan Manley and other members of the small group of textile artists known as 'Running Stitch' mounted the exhibition Wool Quilts, Old and New at Wool House in Melbourne. The ground-breaking show not only raised interest, it created controversy. A few visitors were very hostile that the slapdash workmanship of some of the exhibits did not demonstrate the fine stitchery that they judged to be the most important characteristic of a good quilt. Far more visitors were moved by the display of old quilts, remembering the bed covers of their childhood.

*Q*uiltmakers have come a long way in the last decade. Now, any kind of stitchery is acceptable — as long as it is appropriate to the quilt — although a certain standard of craftsmanship should support a quilt or it will distract from the overall effect.

Not only are galleries showing quilts, they are acquiring them. The works of some of our finest quiltmakers are now in public collections, if not on permanent display.

BOOKS AND MAGAZINES

The rise in popularity of quiltmaking in Australia has been reflected in the increase in the number of quilts pictured in national magazines. Indeed, the magazines have done much to spread the word. Now, hardly any issue of a craft magazine is complete without a quilt, often featured on the cover. The widespread appeal of these publications *popularises quiltmaking* and makes it accessible in the smallest town.

The first Australian magazine devoted to quiltmaking, Down Under Quilts, *began in 1988.*

During the 1970s and 1980s, most of the quiltmaking books and magazines available in Australia came from the United States, with a few standards from Britain. Driven by overseas trends, as represented in these books, and taught by overseas tutors, there has been a succession of recognisable styles in Australian quiltmaking. The formal medallion style, popularised by Jinny Beyer in the late 1970s, with its carefully calculated borders, was overtaken by the scrap look, promoted by Judy Martin. Roberta Horton's less formal approach to plaids and stripes removed the emphasis on precision in cutting out fabric details and introduced a less predictable, more playful element.

Two trends influenced by overseas publications are evident today: firstly, the subtle shading effect achieved by Deidre Amsden in Britain and Canberra quiltmaker Judy Turner and, secondly, fine appliqué in the style of last century's 'Baltimore Album' quilts.

THE FIRST TO CHAMPION AN AUSTRALIAN QUILTING IDENTITY WAS CANBERRA QUILTMAKER MARGARET ROLFE WITH HER ENORMOUSLY POPULAR *AUSTRALIAN PATCHWORK* (CURRY O'NEIL 1985), FEATURING NATIVE ANIMALS AND FLOWERS IN HER ORIGINAL DESIGNS.

She also wrote a history of the art, Patchwork Quilts in Australia (Greenhouse Press 1987), with the

DETAIL FROM A QUILT MADE FROM OLD SUITING SAMPLES BY ELIZABETH GARRETT, CIRCA 1900, WHICH IS TYPICAL OF SUCH QUILTS OF THE PERIOD (POWERHOUSE MUSEUM)

assistance of a grant from the Australia Council. Many smaller books have followed. Her books are also available in the United States where she has done much to promote an Australian identity in quiltmaking.

There have been a number of other significant quilt-making books written in Australia: Deborah Brearley has published several books of quilt designs inspired by the local environment. Barbara Macey and Susan Denton's Quiltmaking *(Thomas Nelson Australia 1988) features photographs of many quilts by leading Australian quiltmakers, as well as covering general instructions on how to make quilts and sections by both women on techniques that they have developed. Dianne Finnegan's book* Piece by Piece, The Complete Book of Quiltmaking *(Simon & Schuster 1990) also features the work of many Australians, as does her other book* The Quilters' Kaleidoscope *(Simon & Schuster 1992) which examines the evolution of different styles, illustrated by old and new quilts. Besides these, there is an expanding list of books covering more specific topics.*

TEACHING

The influence of teachers has been very significant in spreading information about the techniques of quiltmaking and, more recently, about design and colour. Ten or fifteen years ago, many of those teaching in Australia would have learned their craft while resident in the United States, where quiltmaking had undergone a renaissance prior to the American bicentenary in 1976. Trudy Billingsley is one of the most influential of these, having taught several leading quiltmakers and teachers.

SPRING BOUQUETS
WENDY SMITH
FROM QUILT AUSTRALIA '88

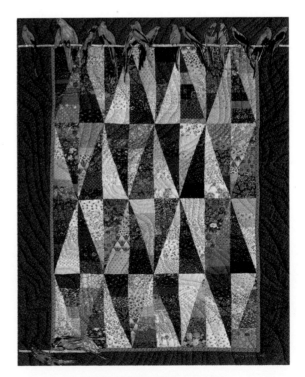

A SUNBURNT COUNTRY
JUDY TURNER
FROM QUILT AUSTRALIA '88

Narelle Grieve was another who learned quiltmaking in the United States. She is an accredited teacher with both the National Quilting Association USA and The Quilters' Guild in Australia. She has introduced many newcomers to the beauty of fine hand-quilting.

Now the pool of teachers has widened. Students of the original wave of teachers have also started teaching Others, inspired by the craft and encouraged by the need for teachers, have begun giving classes.

Besides local classes run by quilt shops, evening colleges and local quilt groups, a growing number of workshops are being offered, with the participants living in, such as The Australasian Quilt Symposium. This was first organised by Barbara Meredith in 1988 and became an annual event of national significance, with tutors drawn from across the country as well as from overseas. It was a vital training ground for quiltmakers, as well as providing a venue for regular contact and friendship.

There was a time when tutors were imported from the United States to teach us how to quilt. Now we recognise that there are many fine local teachers and, increasingly, they are travelling around the country giving workshops.

Nevertheless, there will always be a place for 'cross-fertilisation' and, as other countries are more frequently inviting Australian quiltmakers to teach and exhibit, we will continue to reciprocate.

Teaching can also occur on a less formal basis, and this is illustrated by the number of community projects that involve quiltmaking.

Community-based projects across the country have furnished many public places with quilts, depicting scenes of local significance and, incidentally, educating makers and viewers about quilts.

THE STATE GUILDS

The appearance of quilts in magazines, the availability of quiltmaking books, the influence of teachers and the establishment of quiltmaking supply shops all contributed to the ground swell that resulted in the development of statewide guilds.

Canberra Quilters and The West Australian Quilters Association were the first to form, in 1976, and most states had formed guilds by the mid-eighties. Not all quiltmakers are members of state guilds, so membership numbers do not reflect the full participation rate. Some quiltmakers work in isolation, others are content to belong to informal quilting bees or to a local quilting group made up of friends and neighbours.

AS QUILTMAKING GROWS IN POPULARITY, MEMBERSHIP OF THE STATE GUILDS ALSO GROWS. EVEN THOSE WHO DO NOT BELONG HAVE ACCESS TO GUILD EVENTS AND INFORMATION THROUGH FRIENDS AND PUBLICATIONS.

The state guilds have done much to promote quiltmaking by extending the range of educational and exhibiting opportunities, as well as providing a vehicle for the spreading of information through regular newsletters and magazines.

The state guilds are voluntary organisations. With the enthusiasm and commitment of their elected committees, they are able to provide a wide range of services to

their members. Each state has different needs, but most organise
exhibitions; conduct regular gen-
eral meetings with speakers; hold workshops; maintain a
library of quilt-related books, magazines, videos, etc;
and offer teacher accreditation and quilt valuations.

Several guilds organise annual 'challenges' where
quiltmakers are encouraged to make quilts with the
theme and dimensions specified. These travel over the
next twelve months to all the groups requesting them.
For small country towns, displaying the quilts keeps
them in touch with trends and other quiltmakers.

The guilds realise the importance of a library service
for isolated quiltmakers. The Quilters Guild of South
Australia provides cartons of books for its
country groups on a rotating basis. The
Quilters' Guild in Sydney offers a mail
order library service to all members. These
are popular and widely used services for
both city and country members.

In 1993, an innovative development of
The Quilters' Guild was to sponsor an
annual scholarship. This is awarded to a
quiltmaker to develop and/or achieve personal goals in patchwork and quilting.
Greg Somerville, from the Blue Mountains
in New South Wales, was the inaugural
winner of the scholarship, followed in 1994 by Western
Australian, Wendy Lugg.

**THINKING THERE WAS ONLY
ONE WAY I WAS STUCK**
GREG SOMERVILLE
FROM QUILTS COVERING AUSTRALIA

AFTER THE RAIN
WENDY LUGG
FROM QUILT AUSTRALIA '88

**ALLUSION
OF A QUILT**
(DETAIL) BY
DIANNE FIRTH

Although there is no national guild, The Australian Council of Quilters was formed in 1993 to provide a network between states to facilitate information exchange on a range of national issues. The first national conference was hosted by The Quilters' Guild in 1991 and since then annual meetings of all state guilds have been held in Melbourne, Canberra and Adelaide.

EXHIBITIONS

The most widespread influence of the guilds comes through their annual exhibitions. These attract many thousands of viewers and are well supported by their own members, as well as by the general public. The standard of quilts in these exhibitions continues to improve as experience accumulates.

The Sydney Quilt Festival has evolved from the annual members exhibition of The Quilters' Guild, and includes the New Quilt Exhibition, workshops by leading tutors, lectures and many other satellite events.

In any field, the offering of substantial prizes attracts entries and helps to promote excellence. Most state guilds award prizes at their own exhibitions, except for the Australian Capital Territory where the Royal Agricultural and Horticultural Show is the venue for judging quilts. This results in a very strong showing of quilts at an event attended by a wide cross-section of the population.

As the number of women making their own clothes decreases and the profile of quiltmaking is raised, many of these prizes are being sponsored by companies that are pleased to be associated with this growing field. Bernina sewing machines, craft and lifestyle magazines, fabric suppliers and others are sponsoring exhibitions and prizes throughout the country.

Paradoxically, there is an increase in the number of quiltmakers who make art to wear. The move away from the flat rectangular shape of the quilt into the flexible plane of clothing creates new opportunities for innovation. Movement, draping and moulding become considerations in design, fabric choice and technique.

The exhibition Art to Wear at the Craftspace in The Rocks, Sydney, in August 1994, brought together seven textile artists who created an exciting range of clothing. The overall effect was theatrical, full of vitality and high spirits.

The vast repertoire of techniques allowed for great richness in the effects. Fabric was draped, pleated, folded, pieced, appliquéd and quilted. The surfaces were embellished by cut-out work, collage, threadwork, couching, ruching, beading, stuffing, braiding and cording. The range of fabrics was also greater than that generally seen in quilts. Lamé, metallic threads, trims, sequins and buttons all contributed glitter.

Trudy Billingsley curated the collection, contributing several of her own garments.

From 1991, the New Quilt Exhibition, an annual event jointly run by The Quilters' Guild and the Manly Regional Art Gallery and Museum has become the national showcase for contemporary quilts. Each year, the collection travels on from Manly, NSW, to a number of other galleries throughout Australia. This prestigious event provides the opportunity to exhibit for those working beyond the limits of traditional quiltmaking. This juried show was conceived by Anna Brown and Judy Hooworth of The Quilters' Guild.

Michael Pursche, director of the Manly gallery says, 'Art quilts are intended to be displayed on walls and exist within the critical framework of contemporary· Australian practice and aesthetics'.

Dianne Firth's 'Allusion of a Quilt' is a timely example from the 1994 exhibition. The structure of a quilt is maintained, but the sashes stand out as veins on a background net, rather like a decomposing leaf. About it, Dianne wrote that she wished 'to imply all the characteristics of a quilt without being a quilt, to evoke all the references of a quilt, while capturing transparency'.

One-off exhibitions have also proved popular. In 1988, the Australian Forestry Development Industry sponsored an exhibition of quilts and woodwork. This coincided with a world conference on forestry development in Albury-Wodonga, eliciting an exciting response to the forestry theme. In 1994, the Riddoch Regional Art Gallery in Mount Gambier, South Australia, chose quilts as the medium for an exhibition whose theme was based on the history of the area.

The prestigious Tamworth National Fibre Exhibition's annual acquisitive prize has been won by quiltmaker Ruth Stoneley who has also won a Churchill Fellowship to study quiltmaking overseas.

A SAMPLING OF QUILTS AT THE 1994 MEMBERS' EXHIBITION (TOP), IMAGINATION AND INNOVATION AT 'ART TO WEAR' (CENTRE), CONTEMPORARY QUILTS ON SHOW AT MANLY (BELOW)

Collaboration between quiltmaker and artist was the basis of Quilted Visions, under the auspices of The Quilters Guild of South Australia and the Arts Council of South Australia. Artists working in various media designed a work that could be interpreted in patchwork. The finished works of both the artist and the quiltmaker were exhibited in the foyer of the Adelaide Festival Centre in 1988.

Threads of Journeys, Australian Quilt Textiles was curated by Jan Irvine for the Cultural Relations Branch of the Department of Foreign Affairs and Trade, and travelled extensively through Europe, Asia, the Pacific and Canada during 1991 to 1993. The accompanying catalogue, illustrating all the quilts, is a permanent record of the collection.

QUILT AUSTRALIA '88 WAS AN AMBITIOUS PROGRAM WHICH INCLUDED THE FIRST NATIONAL QUILT EXHIBITION IN SYDNEY. THIS EXHIBITION HAD THREE PARTS: CONTEMPORARY AUSTRALIAN QUILTS, HISTORIC AUSTRALIAN QUILTS AND BANNERS MADE BY SCHOOL CHILDREN.

There was also a separate collection of small quilts that toured the country for five years.

The main exhibition displayed ninety-six quilts selected from entries received from all over Australia. This was a juried show with a specific theme. The quilts were to have an Australian emphasis, with the categories including patriotic, political, personal, natural and traditional. This stretched many quiltmakers to think beyond the traditional patterns to design their first original quilt. Many commented on the sense of challenge and excitement that the exhibition created.

An historical collection, curated by Margaret Rolfe, drew together for the first time thirty-one quilts from private and public collections. To date, it is the only comprehensive exhibition of representative examples of Australian quilt styles throughout the last two centuries – a major achievement by Margaret.

The Schools Banner Project, a selection of quilts made by schoolchildren, was organised by Yvonne Line. The children's quilts subsequently toured extensively and were featured in an exhibition in Parliament House, New South Wales.

Another exhibition, Quilts Covering Australia, came to be known more familiarly as the 'Suitcase Exhibition'. Collections of eight or nine small quilts with accompanying documentation and hanging systems travelled around the country in suitcases. The exhibition was initiated and curated by Jan Irvine, with the assistance of a grant from the Australia Council. Jan also wrote the accompanying book, Australian Quilts: the People and Their Art (Simon & Schuster 1989).

The quilts were exhibited continually from 1988 to

1993 and travelled to every state and territory of Australia. In those five years, it is estimated that one hundred and fifty thousand people in rural Australia saw the exhibitions.

Itineraries were organised by the state Arts Councils, ensuring that even the most remote and isolated areas had an equal opportunity to host these high-quality exhibitions. The exhibitions travelled everywhere: Bourke, Longreach, Caloundra, Kangaroo Island, Weipa, Geraldton, Gladstone, Alice Springs, Wangaratta, Gilgandra, Nyngan, Katherine and all points between.

By mounting these national exhibitions and, even more importantly, by documenting them in books, The Quilters' Guild has raised the status of quiltmaking in Australia. As the 'Suitcase Exhibition' neared the end of its tour, The Quilters' Guild was encouraged to initiate another touring exhibition, Colours of Australia.

COLOURS OF AUSTRALIA

Colour is the single most striking feature of Australian quilts; their strength of colour, range of hues and exciting combinations set them apart from quilts from other countries. The theme, Colours of Australia, was intended to provide a wide spectrum of possible interpretations which embody colours and symbolism that are uniquely Australian.

Colours of Australia was a very inspiring choice. Quiltmakers were invited to interpret the theme, using either traditional or contemporary techniques. Entries were received from as far afield as Perth, Western Australia; Yeronga, Queensland; Gove, Northern

Territory; Mount Gambier, South Australia; as well as from New Zealand and the United Kingdom.

The environment was a popular choice for the interpretation of the theme. Community issues, particularly multicultural diversity, were also represented, and colour itself was the starting point for many designs. Political statements were made about the country's history, republicanism, debate about a new flag, war and atomic testing. Some designs were straightforward while others were satirical or poignant.

OVERWHELMINGLY, PARTICIPANTS CHOSE TO DEVELOP THEIR THEME WITH AN ORIGINAL DESIGN, RATHER THAN BY USING A TRADITIONAL PATTERN. IN THE 1990s, IT IS APPARENT THAT QUILTMAKERS HAVE CONFIDENCE IN THEIR MASTERY OF THE MEDIUM AND OF THE DESIGN PROCESS.

THE 1994 COLOURS OF AUSTRALIA ENTRIES EXHIBITION AT THE SYDNEY OPERA HOUSE

CONVICTS AND SOLDIERS
(DETAIL) BY VAL NADIN

FROM A DISTANCE
(DETAIL) BY KERRY GADD

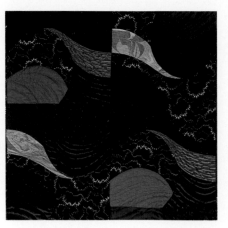

RHYTHM OF THE REEF
(DETAIL) BY ELIZABETH BREN

Among the participants are many well-established quilt-makers, as well as those who had never previously exhibited, or even made a quilt before, attesting to the vitality and widening popularity of quiltmaking in Australia. They are from large centres and from the out-back, as well as from women of all ages. Although a few men entered quilts for consideration, it happened that none were selected, reflecting the dominance of women in this field.

These quilts are intended to be viewed on a wall, so they are more consciously art works, rather than a functional quilt to be used on a bed. All the quilts had to be 90 cm x 125 cm (35½ in x 49 in) and they could be either vertical or horizontal. Traditionally, most quilts are made for beds and are therefore longer than they are wide. Colours of Australia presented an opportunity for quiltmakers to work with a horizontal format which was taken up by about one-third of the quiltmakers.

The quilts had to conform to certain conditions because they were to travel for several years. To survive the constant handling, they could not be fragile, ephemeral pieces. Nevertheless, within these constraints, the content, style and range of techniques shows the diversity and maturity of the state of the art of quilt-making in Australia today.

DESIGN STRUCTURE

In general, the quilts show original designs, covering the whole surface of the quilt, rather than the traditional grid of repeating blocks.

Where traditional patterns are used, they are not used in their original format. For instance, the traditional Beggars' Block is almost unrecognisable when it is elongated into a rectangle and adapted by Val Nadin to fit the required dimensions. She interpreted the block in a non-representational manner to fit her quilt, 'Convicts and Soldiers – First Settlement' (page 36). Colour, shape and fabric were all employed to convey the theme of the two classes of first settlers sent out to Australia from Britain in the late eighteenth century.

Elizabeth Bren used a rectangular block for her quilt, 'Rhythm of the Reef' (page 37), in which the curved piecing captures the swirl of water. The varied textures of the fabrics create the impression of differing depths of water, dappled shallows, and light reflecting on the surface. The quilt has the look of aerial photography in which the image is reduced to a pattern of coloured shapes.

Bronwen Gibbs (page 65) breaks up her colour study of sand and surf with blocks and sashes, but the colours spill over from one to the other, so that the block unit emerges and disappears. Pat Hagan plays with the convention of the block quilt, when she uses a grid of block-shaped pillows for her resting babies (page 39).

Dale Brown's quilt, 'A Land of Volunteers — True Oz Spirit' (page 54), has an original format, with several sections representing different emergency services. Dale treats it as a sampler quilt — an opportunity to try out new techniques where the blocks are rectangular and not in a conventional grid.

Kerry Gadd takes an aerial view of the whole continent for her quilt, 'From a Distance' (page 59). She has divided the quilt into units, but not the regular grid of a traditional block quilt. Her grid is distorted in a very complex way, so that no two blocks are the same. The stepped effect of the Log Cabin further fragments the distorted grid.

COLOUR

The distribution of colours on Kerry's quilt approximates the landscape and the temperature zones of the continent. Starting in the centre, the yellows represent the desert sands, then hot red radiates out in all directions. The edges change to the cooler greens, blues and turquoises of vegetation and water of our coastal fringe.

Colours were also a starting point for Anna Brown's quilt, 'Origins' (page 60) — the blue of the sky, the tropical colours of the Barrier Reef and the strong earth

colours of the outback are all representative. The simple design of a pieced central panel, surrounded by a single border, emphasises the colour and quilting. Quilted spirals, the most ancient of symbols, recall the original Koori inhabitants of the land. In the central panel, quilted leaves represent the natural environment and, above these, vertical forms unfold into stars and the sky.

The image is not so immediately obvious in Larraine Scouler's quilt, 'Queensland's Blue Lightning' (page 57), which is based on the colours of blue opal. The brilliant, iridescent quality of the boulder opal is portrayed in light reflective fabrics. These contrast with the dull brown of the weathered rock surface. Some of the fabrics were overdyed to achieve the required sequence of colours. Strips were sewn together in bands of colour, then cut across and offset. This technique is known as 'Seminole'. The offsetting and rearrangement of the sequence expresses the prismatic character of the opal.

ORIGINS (DETAIL) BY ANNA BROWN FEATURING THE EVOCATIVE HAND-QUILTED SPIRALS OF KOORI LEGEND

SYMBOLS AND ICONS

There are some Koori (Aboriginal) symbols that recur in several quilts. These are not appropriated from their source, rather the Aboriginality has been expressed in symbolism, imagery and palette, such as the spirals worked in reverse appliqué by Dale Brown in her quilt, A 'Land of Volunteers – True Oz Spirit' (page 54).

DETAILS FROM **A LAND OF VOLUNTEERS –TRUE OZ SPIRIT** BY DALE BROWN (LEFT) AND **HOLLOW MOUNTAIN LAYERS** BY SUSAN CUNNINGHAM (RIGHT)

Hands are also featured, suggesting a helping hand as well as that common feature of Koori rock painting. The hand outline is also quilted in Susan Cunningham's quilt, 'Hollow Mountain Layers' (page 41).

A collaboration between two white women, Catherine Brown and Barbara Philp, and two Koori sisters, Wuyuwa (Bronwyn) and Yananymul (Thelma) Mununggurr, produced the quilt named 'North-east Arnhemland Billabong' (page 70). When she heard about the exhibition, Catherine saw it as an opportunity to work with Bronwyn and Thelma and, through this partnership, draw on both cultures and art forms. The story of the quilt is told on page 70.

THE WOMEN WORKED TOGETHER FOR TWO MONTHS, SITTING CROSS-LEGGED ON THE FLOOR, PAINTING THE DESIGN ONTO UNTREATED CANVAS STRETCHED OVER A FRAME, THEN QUILTING IT.

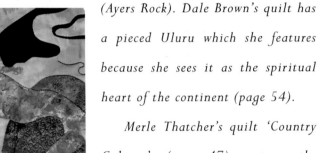

Certain familiar icons are repeated in many of the quilts; for example, there are several images of Uluru (Ayers Rock). Dale Brown's quilt has a pieced Uluru which she features because she sees it as the spiritual heart of the continent (page 54).

Merle Thatcher's quilt 'Country Colours', (page 47) captures the Australian landscape with gum trees, animals and birds, and has an inset of Uluru appliquéd in the heart of the quilt.

Sue Wademan's quilt, 'Red Rock – Uluru' (page 61), concentrates on the rock with the red colour glowing in the vastness of the blue sky. The use of shiny silk demands attention and the threads and frayed edges of the strip-pieced foreground gives the impression of grasses and indistinct edges in the shimmering heat. Sue calls her technique 'painting with threads'. Metallic threads add to the richness of the land, while antique beads twinkle, breaking up the vast expanse of sky. The asymmetrical border is an Aboriginal fabric, reinforcing the fact that Uluru is the spiritual centre of Koori culture.

Helen Howe's quilt, 'Australia – the Eye of the World is upon You' (page 40), is crammed with Australian images, including the national and Aboriginal flags in the corners.

THE LANDSCAPE, NATURAL
AND CONSTRUCTED

A montage of Australian images appears in Roslyn Moules's quilt, 'Red Earth, Blue Sky and Sun' (page 63). The dominance of the horizon suggests the wide open land. The quilt underlines this emphasis on the flat horizon that dominates the Australian landscape. Buildings curving upwards, the Sydney Harbour Bridge and the Sydney Opera House represent the constructed environment. The quilted line drawings fill the space in a balanced design, representing the breadth of the Australian environment.

Sand and surf are archetypal national images and their golds and blues are the colours that Bronwen Gibbs calls on to represent Australia in her quilt, 'Hidden Landscapes' (page 65). She Gocco-printed and dyed her fabrics to bring to mind waves of rolling surf and undulating marram grass, photocopying and overprinting the grasses to further enhance the image. Fragmenting the image and setting it into blocks abstracts it from reality while placing it firmly in the patchwork tradition of blocks separated by sashes.

Dianne Jones lives in a national park, so she had to look no further then her own back yard for inspiration. In three panels of her quilt, 'Up ... Down ... All Around' (page 53), she illustrates the leaves of the canopy, the mountains and rocks and, on a more intimate scale, the tiny flowers on the ground. The use of netting has a softening effect on the colours. Dianne employs a wide range of techniques to achieve her effects: hand-dyeing and painting, appliqué, piecing, machine-quilting and embroidery.

HIDDEN LANDSCAPES
BRONWEN GIBBS

UP... DOWN... ALL AROUND
DIANNE JONES

To Eileen Campbell, the magpies' morning song is the essence of Australia. Her quilt, 'Spring Morning' (page 43), with its magpies in full cry, is a realistic composition, evoking the beauty of the natural world. Fine machine-stitchery defines the details.

Birds also inspired Wendelee Weis in designing her quilt, 'Parrots in the Trees — Colour and Movement' (page 58). She has captured the movement and flash of colours of the rainbow lorikeets, eastern and paleface rosellas that fly past her home.

With no formal instruction, Wendelee did not plan the quilt on paper but jumped in, cutting out the fabrics and stitching them down so that the design emerged as she went: ruched spirals of unfolding colours spin off into ribbons, then lines of stitching stretch across velvets, silks and satins.

Perhaps, if she had had formal instruction, she would have realised that these techniques and fabrics are often considered too difficult for a beginner quiltmaker to handle!

Pam Winsen sees her quilt, 'Crabs and Mangroves' (page 75), as the first of a series, starting at the coast and progressing across the land. Confronted with the decision of how to represent the colours of Australia, she

'Hollow Mountain Layers' by Susan Cunningham (page 41) also portrays the textures of nature. Found fabrics were hand-painted and printed with fabric paint and disperse dyes to give the impression of rock surfaces and layers. Calico, organdie, chintz, plain cottons and furnishing fabrics are all used to convey the impression of a landscape. Layers of meaning are built up: rock strata with their great geological age have Aboriginal rock paintings superimposed on them — a layer from a more recent age; stipple-quilting in contrasting thread extends the image of a lichen-covered rock surface; large hand-quilting enhances the textured fabrics, continuing the strata from printed to plain fabric. Deep black reverse-appliqué lines suggest deep chasms and water courses. The mystery of Hollow Mountain has been caught in this quilt.

narrowed her choice to two elements, crabs and mangrove trees, then repeated them as rows of pattern. She hand-dyed cottons and chiffons to get the variations in the colours of water and trees.

THE ORANGE CRABS SING AGAINST THE COMPLEMENTARY COLOUR OF THE WATER; THE TRAILS AND CLUMPS OF THREAD CLINGING TO THE MANGROVE TREES GIVE A REALISTIC TEXTURE.

Englishwoman Annette Claxton's memories of a recent trip through the Kimberleys and the Bungle Bungles up to Broome and Coral Bay in Western Australia are captured in abstract form in 'NWWA' (North-west Western Australia) (page 56). The red earth, strata of the spectacular Bungle Bungle range, the radiating leaves of a palm tree and the shapes of gorges and creeks are all represented. To the west is the coast, with fish and sea next to earth. Spotted fabrics make reference to Aboriginal art, as does the snake image.

Jennifer Lewis has also called on her extensive knowledge of the outback for her quilt design, gleaned from many trips in a four-wheel drive vehicle. The name of the quilt is, in fact, the number plate of her car, EIW 448 (page 62). The towering blocks of colour give a solidity and massiveness to the mountains; their shape is very organic. Prints are only used for vegetation. Jennifer improvises with thread and concentrates on the image. She works by hand and machine, exploiting the characteristics of both. Jennifer uses hand-appliqué for a hard edge, while for softness and texture she machines some raw edges, then frays the fabric so that the threads lie on the surface.

EIW 448
JENNIFER LEWIS

NWWA
ANNETTE CLAXTON

Trees were the subject of two quilts, 'Forest III' by Joy Serwylo (page 50) and 'Bush Textures' by Wendy Lugg (page 52). Both quiltmakers overprinted found fabrics to achieve a range of colours and textures. Joy describes her fabrics as 'cut colours'. Her quilt is a collage, secured by a scribble of machine-stitching. The foreground of leaf litter and low canopy consists of hundreds of pieces of fabric to give density and complexity to the quilt.

Wendy's quilt is a vertical cross section through the bush with slashes of tree trunks. Disparate curtain fabrics are overprinted so that a continuum develops, one fabric merging imperceptibly with the next. They are crazy-patched together so that there is no obvious geometry of piecing to detract from the gradation from back light to canopy. The tree trunks loom and retreat behind the leaves. Her arts training is obvious from her confident handling of texture and light.

Judy Day's quilt, 'Just Leaves' (page 64), is a very traditional quilt, with the beauty of fine handwork. A century-old pattern is given an Australian slant by using over a hundred and fifty different fabrics for the leaves in the colours of the bushland close to Judy's

home. Exquisite hand-appliqué and hand-quilting add to the traditional feeling evoked by the quilt.

The natural landscape is integrated with the constructed environment in 'From Today' by Sandra Burchill (page 46). Sandra uses patchwork fabrics, as well as non-traditional fabrics,

TOORALLIE IN BOMBALA (DETAIL) BY N. GRIEVE

to represent the past and the future. The quilt builds around an Australian-designed-and-made fabric, an Ascraft toile of the first settlement. Ascraft is an innovative Australian company that commissioned fabrics showing historical scenes to be designed and printed for the Bicentenary.

This image is inset into an 'impossible' triangle that celebrates Captain Cook's extraordinary navigational accomplishments in mapping the coast of Australia. Below this, an abstract fabric is quilted to suggest buildings, and a web of lurex surrounds this whole central area, hinting at the future, gradually peeling back to reveal itself, bright with possibilities.

A single building, the Maryborough Railway Station in Victoria, is the focus of another quilt, 'My Ultimate Challenge' (page 42). Anna Alford has brought together the beautiful local building and Australian wildflowers in her quilt design. The wattle border represents not only the floral emblem of Australia, but also the Wattle Festival in Maryborough. All the colours are significant,

JUST LEAVES (DETAIL) BY JUDY DAY

relating to her personal life and to the environment. The embroidered centre of the quilt recalls an earlier era of fine needlework.

Judy Hooworth's abstract quilt, 'Urban Landscape' (page 49), concentrates on one aspect of the constructed environment — road and sewerage works. Saturated colours and arresting patterning, derived from barricades, plastic wrappings and signs, have been transformed into an energetic, geometric quilt.

A complete contrast is found in Narelle Grieve's quilt, 'Toorallie in Bombala' (page 38). This is a wholecloth quilt (the top made of one piece of fabric with no joins). With the absence of any colour or patch-

work, the emphasis is on the quilting and it is an example of fine handwork.

THE WORK HAS THE DELICACY OF AN OLD-FASHIONED QUILT, BUT THE DESIGN WAS DRAWN FROM THE PRESSED-TIN CEILINGS AND WALLS OF AN OLD PICTURE THEATRE.

Close stipple-quilting holds down the background

FROM TODAY (DETAIL) BY SANDRA BURCHILL

areas of the design, giving the raised effect of a pattern in pressed metal.

Alison Muir achieves a contemporary look with semi-abstract shapes and a frayed-edge technique in her quilt, 'Sydney' (page 67). She does not see the quilt as a static work of art, but imagines the fraying increasing over time with handling. The quilt has the almost abstract quality of aerial photography, with large colour blocks of sun, sand and earth, with appliquéd dashes and rectangles for buildings and clumps of green for vegetation. Some are skewed, giving a sense of movement and hurry. Silks evoke the dancing sunlight with their light reflective quality.

TEXT AND TEXTILES

In some quilts, the messages are spelt out more literally. Several quilts incorporate text — hand-written, stencilled or printed on the fabric. They deal with events that raise strong emotions, such as fires, war and nuclear testing.

'Blackened Beauty', Leonie Andrews's quilt (page 71), has a cartographic effect — it looks like a map with features labelled. On closer examination, the traditional Kansas Troubles block underlays islands of apparently burnt fragments, the block pattern providing dynamic movement without drawing attention to the piecing. Plain fabrics incorporate screen-printed newspaper headlines sensationalising the fires. This was one of several quilts submitted with a bushfire theme — a response to the devastating bushfires experienced near Sydney and in other areas of New South Wales in January 1994.

Wendy Holland lives at Mount Wilson in the Blue Mountains, west of Sydney, and watched the fires encroaching. The dramatic changes are captured in her quilt, 'Expired Pyre' (page 69).

USING A LIMITED PALETTE, SHE MAKES AN ABSTRACT STATEMENT ABOUT THE BLACKENED LANDSCAPE, INCORPORATING THE ABORIGINAL SEMI-CIRCULAR MOTIFS TO CONNECT THE LAND WITH ITS PAST AND RECALL ITS GREAT AGE.

On closer examination, the dark tones break up into a surprising number of different blacks, browns and greens, arranged in irregular rows of patches suggestive of fields. Overlapping raw, pinked edges, mother-of-pearl buttons, large quilting stitches and a variety of fabrics all contribute to a subtle textural quality that increases the complexity of the quilt.

BLACKENED BEAUTY
(DETAIL) BY LEONIE ANDREWS

EXPIRED PYRE
(DETAIL) BY WENDY HOLLAND

Texture is also important in Jan Tregoweth's quilt, 'Forest Fury' (page 45). Tucked fabrics are easily identified as trees, twisted and blackened, with the undersides of the tucks in a grey ash colour. The red and yellow stripped background suggests the fire burning in the distance, and the daubs of acrylic paint capture the flames, wind-blown ash and smoke.

Barbara Macey's quilt, 'Flames, Ash, Embers' (page 55) is a bushfire recollected in tranquillity. Twenty-five years ago, Barbara was nearly caught in a bushfire when her clothes were scorched by burning gum leaves, carried

DETAILS FROM **FOREST FURY** (ABOVE) BY JAN TREGOWETH AND **FLAMES, ASH, EMBERS** (INSET) BY BARBARA MACEY, TWO QUILTS WHICH DEAL WITH THE SUBJECT OF BUSHFIRES

in the gale-force winds. The quilt has two distinct parts; the flames of the border surround a paler central panel of ash and embers left in the fire's wake. Gum leaves are scattered across the surface, red hot in the border, ashen in the centre. The whole quilt is comprised of a grid of parallelograms. The order of the grid is interrupted by the crazy patching and the superimposed swirling leaves.

DETAILS FROM **I WAS THINKING IT MIGHT BE A DUST STORM** BY HELEN BROOK (ABOVE), AND **ANZAC** BY MARGARET ROLFE (RIGHT)

THE YEARS THAT WERE THAT SHOULD NEVER HAVE BEEN (DETAIL) BY LARAINE PICKETT

Another kind of catastrophe is captured in Helen Brook's quilt, 'I Was Thinking It Might Be a Dust Storm' (page 44). Helen believes that quiltmaking is a medium through which to address social and personal issues. She has used this opportunity to comment on British atomic testing in the Maralinga area of South Australia in 1956 and 1957. Local inhabitants, mainly Koori, were not warned of the testing and consequently many of them became sick and died. The texts on the quilt recount the first-hand impressions of the Koori, while the name of the quilt is taken from a comment made at the time which summed up their lack of preparedness and their defencelessness.

Like bushfires, war is a recurring theme. In this, her first quilt, 'The Years That Were That Should Never Have Been' (page 73), Laraine Pickett explores the play of light and colour in her tribute to those who served in Vietnam. The colours used are symbolic: red for blood and the Vietcong flag, black for death, yellow for the South Vietnamese flag, and army green for the men who served, all set among jungle green fabric. Military insignia; clothing details, like buttons and pockets; printed and hand-lettered information all draw the viewer into the quilt.

Margaret Rolfe looks at an earlier war in her quilt, 'ANZAC' (page 72). This quilt is a tribute to all the young soldiers who went off to fight in World War I and are remembered on Anzac Day. The red poppies are for the nearly sixty thousand of them who did not return.

Everything in this quilt is meaningful: the use of wool suiting samples in rectangles is reminiscent of early Australian bush quilts, the black border for death and red poppies for remembrance, the backing recalls the calico wrapped around tins of food sent to the soldiers.

The fabric colours used for the rectangles recall not only the colours of men's suits but also the khaki of their military uniforms.

POLITICAL COMMENT

Several quilts comment on current issues and two offer satirical comments on the debate over a new national flag. Judy McDermott's quilt, '... And See Who Salutes' (page 68) has the format of a flag on first viewing, although the meaning of the enormous banana is not immediately clear. On closer inspection, all the elements of the design are telling. In the top left-hand corner, the national flag is deconstructed and, although the seven stars representing states and territories are there, they are not obvious. The central flag floats on a black, yellow and red background – a reference to the Koori flag. The fabrics themselves suggest many different themes – a star-filled night, the word 'OZ' (which Judy wants to be read as 'NO') and Koori-style markings. The overpowering image of the banana is a comment on the state of the economy, suggesting a banana republic.

The title of Nola Gibson's quilt, 'Keep the Aspidistra Flying' (page 51), also suggests a flag. Her work refers back to our English connections, with potted aspidistras conjuring up visions of drawing rooms in Victorian England. The calm, symmetrical arrangement is in stark contrast to Judy's flag. This wholecloth quilt has been airbrushed and the spare, elegant design is enhanced by the detailing of hand-quilting.

Images drawn from the political culture form the basis of Kerrilyn Gavin's light-hearted quilt, 'Under the Big Top' (page 48). The title has a double meaning: it refers to the usual circuses and also to the circus that is our federal parliament (Kerrilyn lives in Canberra, the national capital). The quilt incorporates a number of images: the national flag, parliament house, the ringmaster in the top hat and the grey politicians (some with clowns' faces appliquéd on), surrounded by the colourful masses.

UNDER THE BIG TOP (DETAIL) BY KERRILYN GAVIN (TOP), **'... AND SEE WHO SALUTES'** BY JUDY McDERMOTT (ABOVE)

THE BACK OF THE QUILT '... **AND SEE WHO SALUTES**' BY JUDY McDERMOTT (ABOVE), WITH DETAILS FROM THE BACKS OF **ORIGINS** BY ANNA BROWN (INSET) AND **ANZAC** BY MARGARET ROLFE (RIGHT)

There is always a temptation to touch quilts; they have such tactile appeal. At an exhibition, touching is discouraged, so the backs are not seen. Many of these quilts have wonderful backs, satisfying for the maker and a secret to be shared with the privileged few who handle the quilts while hanging them.

Several quiltmakers clearly intended that the back of their quilts be 'read' as an integral part of the whole. Judy McDermott continues her theme of the banana republic on the back of her quilt. There can be no mistaking her feelings on the subject! A different sort of communication can be found on the back of Margaret Rolfe's quilt, 'ANZAC' (page 72). On the calico backing is written the life story of Frank Rolfe, whose youthful likeness, dressed in ANZAC uniform, appears on the front of the quilt.

SOCIETY

An entirely different mood is evoked in Alysoun Ryves's quilt, 'Summertime' (page 66). She comments that, although politicians wish we had a strong work ethic to boost productivity, we do have a wonderful vacation ethic. Using the medallion style of a central panel surrounded by borders, she portrays the bright, clear colours of summer and casual beach holidays, especially the tropical colours of the Great Barrier Reef. The vacation spirit triumphs, with fish and flowers tumbling out of their borders. The pieced borders do not fit evenly in repeat units, but are truncated, reflecting a more relaxed attitude.

Several quiltmakers made comments on community issues. Multiculturalism is represented by Pat Hagan in her whimsical quilt, 'Made in Australia' (page 39). Set in the traditional format of a block quilt with sashing, nine babies sit or lie on pillows (the blocks), each with a different skin tone, suggesting the variety of ethnic backgrounds in Australia. Fine machine-embroidery gives the babies their facial expressions and anatomical details. Even the silver safety pins are specially made (Pat was a silversmith first and a quiltmaker only latterly). The babies are surrounded by a gum leaf fabric that makes it quite certain where they were made!

The dichotomy of black-and-white Australia and references to the black culture that underpins our national identity are recurring themes in the exhibition. Adina Sullivan's quilt, 'Together in Harmony'

(page 74), represents Australia as two women, one Koori and one of European descent. The two women dance together, the outline of their bodies forming a map of Australia — even the island of Tasmania is included. The echo-quilting in the surrounding fabric suggests waves; the outline-quilting of the brown fabric between the dancers gives the impression of landforms. Even the fabric used for their hair is cleverly chosen to further enhance the differences between the women.

DETAILS FROM **MADE IN AUSTRALIA**
BY PAT HAGAN

DIRECTIONS IN AUSTRALIAN QUILTMAKING

The quilts that have been selected for the Colours of Australia collection exemplify the trends in Australian quiltmaking to the mid-1990s and indicate the directions of future developments.

Quiltmakers have taken the opportunity presented by the Colours of Australia Exhibition to explore new techniques and to express their views on issues of importance. The quilts are a fascinating 'snapshot' of the state of the art in Australia in 1994. They are technically and artistically excellent, and are based firmly in the tradition of quiltmaking.

THE RANGE OF TECHNIQUES AND FABRICS AVAILABLE TO THE MODERN QUILTMAKER HAS NO BOUNDARIES. GONE ARE THE DAYS WHEN HANDWORK REIGNED SUPREME AND A QUILT COULD BE CONDEMNED BY CONSERVATIVE VIEWERS IF IT WAS PIECED OR QUILTED BY MACHINE.

Today, there is a more widespread appreciation of the success of the final product, based on overall impact, regardless of technique. The number of patches, the size of the quilt, the amount of quilting and the hours involved in making the quilt are no longer predictors of success. Quiltmaker Bronwen Gibbs sums it up when she says: 'Technique can be innovative and expressive — a means to an end and not an end in itself'.

The fabric choice demonstrated in these forty quilts extends far beyond the confines of traditional cotton patchwork fabrics. A wide range come from non-traditional sources, such as furnishing samples, curtain fabrics, dressmaking materials and opportunity shops. It is good to see some Australian fabrics being used, instead of a total dependence on imported cottons; several quiltmakers have used Koori fabrics of original design. Special effects have been achieved with a variety of other materials: furnishing fabrics, silks, velvets, synthetics and anything else that contributes to the look they want to achieve.

One of the most outstanding features of this collection is the degree of surface design present in the quilts. Plain and printed fabrics have been used as a starting point for dyeing, overdyeing, printing, silk-screening, marbling and painting.

Some quiltmakers painted and drew onto the fabric, rather than using the traditional approach of piecing and appliquéing different fabrics together to build up the design. Other quiltmakers have added colour on top of the patchwork to further develop their theme. Jan Tregoweth (page 45), for example, overpainted the flames, smoke and embers of a bushfire, combining this technique with patchwork, so that the painting is an integral part of the image.

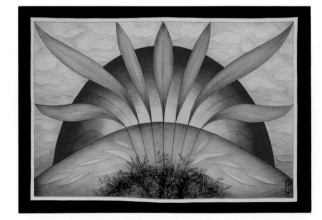

KEEP THE ASPIDISTRA FLYING
NOLA GIBSON

DYEING AND OVERDYEING HAS EXTENDED THE QUILTMAKER'S PALETTE, CREATING NEW COLOURS AND TEXTURES ON FABRICS WHICH CAN BE USED IN COMBINATION WITH FOUND FABRICS.

Increasingly, quiltmakers are experimenting with materials and techniques. Machine-stitchery and threads are more creatively used. The quilt is not only being machine-pieced and appliquéd, but the quilt-maker is skilfully using the sewing machine as a tool, achieving a variety of embroidery and quilting effects.

Metallic thread, used in combination with the sewing machine, enjoys a new prominence, so not only the light reflective materials but also the thread of the stitching lines catches the light and adds sparkle.

Seams in piecing and in appliqué are not always turned under neatly. Sometimes, the raw edges of the fabrics are left exposed and frayed for effect. The ends of threads are not necessarily concealed. On occasion, they are left hanging from the surface of the quilt to become a design element in their own right.

Fabric manipulation adds another dimension to the surface of some quilts. Not only is the fabric pieced and layered, it is also tucked, ruched and folded. Occasionally the completed patchwork is covered by net to soften and, perhaps, to blur the outlines. Embellishments, such as buttons and beads, are also added for texture and effect.

The quilting stitch is used in many guises for different effects. Hand-quilting gives a soft, traditional effect, but longer stitches and thicker thread increase the impact, and different coloured threads add to the

design. Machine-quilting produces a harder line and can be more or less obvious, depending on whether it follows the outline of the shapes or draws a new design in the open area. The variety of quilting techniques is a conspicuous feature of the collection.

RED EARTH, BLUE SKY AND SUN (DETAIL) BY ROSLYN MOULES SHOWING THE CREATIVE USE OF MACHINE-QUILTING

RED ROCK-ULURU (DETAIL) BY SUE WADEMAN SHOWING THE COMBINING OF EMBELLISHMENTS, MACHINE-QUILTING AND COLLAGE

THESE QUILTS ARE OFTEN AUTOBIOGRAPH-
ICAL AND SOMETIMES TOPICAL. THEY DEAL
WITH PLACES AND ISSUES OF SIGNIFIC-
ANCE TO THE MAKERS. THE VARIETY OF
INTERPRETATIONS OF THE THEME REFLECT
THE DIVERSITY OF THE MAKERS, THEIR
INTERESTS, PERCEPTIONS OF NATURE, AND
THEIR CULTURAL BACKGROUNDS.

Landscapes predominate. As Roslyn Moules notes: 'Australian quiltmakers are expressing the vast choice of colours and shapes in our landscape and lifestyle'. Many of the quilts are pictorial, with easily recognisable images, but some are semi-abstract and a few are totally abstract. Organic forms from nature feature more often than geometric patterns. Symbolism is important, and there is an increased confidence in the use of Australian iconography.

The formats are also diverse within the constraints of the required size and shape. There is a bias towards whole-surface designs, although many of these are original designs, rather than copies or adaptations of traditional patterns. The traditional block-repeat quilt is conspicuous by its scarcity, and borders, when added, are an integral design feature of the quilt.

In fact, the quilts capture a whole range of moods and emotions, varying from whimsical, through satirical and thoughtful to expansive and relaxed. While the earth tones of Koori culture are well represented, the quilts include all the colours of the rainbow and both ends of the grey scale. Compared to the colours in quilts from other countries, there is clearly a focus on colour here. The adventurous combinations, the saturation of hues and the emphasis on this element in the design of the quilts is not limited to this collection. It is a feature of Australian quiltmaking.

Quiltmaking is in a relatively early stage of development in this country. It has gathered momentum as the numbers of craftspeople and textile artists, making both functional and art quilts, increase. Opportunities for showing and selling work have expanded.

Publications have multiplied and the quilting guilds have extended their range of services. All of this leads to widespread public awareness of quiltmaking and the growing enthusiasm is supported by a nationwide growth in teaching and learning. The high standard of teaching is reflected in a widespread technical proficiency.

URBAN LANDSCAPE (DETAIL) BY JUDY HOOWORTH

This collection includes names not previously known in Australian quiltmaking circles. Indeed, it was a new medium for several of the makers like Pat Hagan and Laraine Pickett. Adina Sullivan comments on the emergence of wonderful textile artists in quiltmaking, and looks forward to greater things when more barriers are knocked down as they explore different directions. As she says, '… and we've only just begun!'.

Quilts are material documents of our culture, of our personal and community lives, and the makers are exploring many different directions rather than converging. The quilts in the Colours of Australia Exhibition glory in this variety, giving an impression of confidence, diversity, energy, experimentation and progress.

THESE FORTY QUILTS REFLECT THE BEST IN QUILTMAKING IN AUSTRALIA TODAY. COLOURS OF AUSTRALIA PROVIDED AN OPPORTUNITY FOR SELF-EXPRESSION, WHICH WAS INTERPRETED WITH GOOD DESIGN AND EXECUTED WITH EXCELLENT CRAFTSMANSHIP.

Many quiltmakers feel free of the constraints of tradition, which allows them to be creative and explore any avenue. Pam Winsen sees quiltmaking in Australia as very healthy, with 'exciting concepts and excellent execution'. Helen Howe expresses it exuberantly as 'growing all the time, in all directions, bursting at the seams with creativity and ideas'. Wendy Lugg sums it up by saying that our 'quiltmaking has a vitality born of the Australian tradition of improvisation'.

DIANNE FINNEGAN

SYDNEY (DETAIL) BY ALISON MUIR

PARROTS IN THE TREES – COLOUR AND MOVEMENT (DETAIL) BY WENDELEE WEIS

Following the success of the Suitcase Exhibition (Quilts Covering Australia), The Quilters' Guild, with Karen Fail as president, embarked on the development of a second national tour to commence in 1995. The quilts featured here make up that exhibition known as Colours of Australia.

Colours of Australia was quickly established as a title with vision; a concept to inspire quiltmakers everywhere; a theme to extend the creativity of quilt artists; a chance to explore and express ideas and feelings; a forum to show the directions in Australian quiltmaking.

This tour is directed at fostering a number of the Guild's aims: promoting the art and craft of quilt-making, encouraging good design and technique in either traditional or contemporary work, and providing opportunities for quiltmakers to reach a wider audience through both the tour and the accompanying book. For individual quiltmakers, such exposure is virtually unattainable elsewhere.

Two years in the planning, Colours of Australia has evolved as an ambitious project. From the preliminary publicity to reach quiltmakers throughout Australia (Guild members and non-members alike), to the exhibition of entries at The Sydney Opera House in August 1994, and finally the tour

INTRODUCING THE COLOURS OF AUSTRALIA

itself from early 1995, enthusiasm for the project has been unquestionable. The commitment of the voluntary organising committee was buoyed by the support from everyone along the way.

Four self-contained exhibitions of ten quilts each are now touring Australia, wending their way throughout the countryside on itineraries arranged by the Arts Council in each state. Remote and isolated communities have the same opportunities to host the exhibitions as bigger regional centres, such is the nature of the Arts Council network. Venues and locations range from public foyers, shopping centres, libraries, civic spaces and schools, allowing unlimited public access. People will purposefully seek out the exhibitions or unwittingly be exposed to them, as they go about their daily routine. In this way, those not previously familiar with quilts as works of art will be initiated into this increasingly popular art form.

As the tour progresses, each of the exhibitions will rotate around Australia until the conclusion in 1999, when it is estimated that several hundred thousand privileged viewers will have seen and enjoyed Colours of Australia.

MARGARET WRIGHT *President 1994 The Quilters' Guild*

The traditional 'Beggar's Block' provides the basis for my quilt, although the traditional form has been changed and distorted. I have employed considerable symbolism in my choice of materials and colour, using black and white stripes, arrows and sacking to suggest the clothing of convicts of the early European settlement. The jackets and crossed bandoliers of the soldiers are represented by the colours red and white, while the use of silk hints at military decorations.

VAL NADIN

Pennant Hills, New South Wales

CONVICTS AND SOLDIERS – FIRST SETTLEMENT
MATERIALS: SILK, SACKING,
COTTON, POLYESTER
TECHNIQUES: MACHINE-PIECING,
MACHINE-QUILTING

RHYTHM OF THE REEF
MATERIALS: COTTON, SYNTHETIC,
SATIN, HAND-MARBLED SILK,
POLYESTER BATTING
TECHNIQUES: MACHINE-PIECING,
HAND-QUILTING, MACHINE-QUILTING

The Great Barrier Reef, with its varied depths of colour, banded reefs, swirling surf and dappled shallows, shows a quilt-like quality in aerial photography.

My quilt reflects this, capturing the feel of the Reef from the sky. I introduced new textures and techniques to my work, gaining inspiration from the textured fabric in a mother-of-the-bride dress from a secondhand clothing shop, and succeeded in taming various shades of aqua satins and synthetics for my complex curved piecing design.

ELIZABETH BREN
Ballarat, Victoria

At Bombala in New South Wales is a wonderful old picture theatre which now houses The Toorallie Wool Mills. The knitted garments were just wonderful, but the pressed tin on the walls and ceiling of the building took my breath away.

With a penchant for wholecloth quilts, I had to transform those wonderful designs on the tin into a quilt, using stipple-quilting at the end to achieve the pressed-tin effect.

NARELLE GRIEVE
St Ives, New South Wales

TOORALLIE IN BOMBALA
MATERIALS: SYNTHETIC SILK ('NARELLE' FABRIC),
POLYESTER BATTING, COTTON BACKING
TECHNIQUES: WHOLECLOTH WORK, HAND-QUILTING,
STIPPLE-QUILTING

The theme Colours of Australia really captured my imagination. I thought about multiculturalism and the different people now in our society and, of course, their babies. With real babies as models (photos only), I fashioned my nine little people to rest on pillows, creating a three-dimensional effect. The babies' faces are recognisable by their mothers but, unfortunately, I got the gender of some of them wrong.

With limited experience in textiles and classing myself as a non-sewer, I battled with new techniques, learning to love the freedom of machine-quilting as I went along.

PAT HAGAN

Unley, South Australia

MADE IN AUSTRALIA
MATERIALS: COTTON, POLYCOTTON, LACE, COTTON BATTING
TECHNIQUES: APPLIQUE, EMBROIDERY, PAINTING, SOLDERING SILVER SAFETY PINS

On a backdrop of colours celebrating our lifestyle in the sunny outdoors, my quilt includes all of those recognisable icons that are uniquely Australian. With Sydney Olympics 2000 just around the corner, and the world's fascination with our flora and fauna, I was overwhelmed with ideas to include in my design. I chose my favourites, including the Aboriginal flag in the corners of the quilt, capturing something of the essence of Australia. The world is watching you, Australia, and waits for the year 2000 to unfurl.

HELEN HOWE
Pakenham, Victoria

AUSTRALIA – THE EYE OF THE WORLD IS UPON YOU
MATERIALS: COTTON, SILK, POLYESTER BATTING, EMBROIDERY THREADS, ISAFIL NYLON FOR QUILTING
TECHNIQUES: MACHINE-PIECING, MACHINE-APPLIQUE, MACHINE-EMBROIDERY, MACHINE-QUILTING

COLOURS OF AUSTRALIA 40

HOLLOW MOUNTAIN LAYERS
MATERIALS: CALICO, ORGANDIE,
CHINTZ, COTTON
TECHNIQUES: HAND-PAINTING,
HAND-PRINTING, APPLIQUE,
MACHINE-EMBROIDERY,
FREE MACHINE-QUILTING

In the Grampians, Victoria, is the mysterious and haunting Hollow Mountain. I wanted to explore the many varied layers present there — the geological layers, the textural external rocks, and the remnants of Aboriginal presence.

My quilt captures something of this intriguing area with its caves, chasm, rich layers of colours, surreal rock formations and patterns.

SUSAN CUNNINGHAM

Stawell, Victoria

So much of Australia's architectural heritage deserves to be celebrated.

For my quilt, I have chosen the Maryborough Railway Station, a very beautiful building, and surrounded it with wild flowers and wattle. Here in Maryborough, wattle is the focus for The Wattle Festival, held annually, as well as being the nation's floral emblem. The colours of my life surround the station, revealing a dark side with seven flowers (children) to brighten the gloom, and the colours of sun, drought, rain and trees reaching out to the four corners surrounded by the colour of the sea.

ANNA ALFORD
Maryborough, Victoria

MY ULTIMATE CHALLENGE
MATERIALS: COTTON, AIDA CLOTH, EMBROIDERY THREADS
TECHNIQUES: MACHINE-PIECING, HAND-APPLIQUE, BLACKWORK

While overseas, one of the things I missed most was the song of the magpies in the early morning. To me, it is truly the essence of everything Australian: sunshine-filled mornings, the noises of the bush and freedom, the contrast of black and white against the soft tones of the bush.

My quilt celebrates the magpie, and follows a series of quilts using machine-appliqué techniques with birds, flowers and other small creatures. I draw the animals from pictures and the flowers are designed as I go along to fit in with the overall effect of the quilt.

EILEEN CAMPBELL
Kew, Victoria

SPRING MORNING
MATERIALS: COTTON
TECHNIQUES: MACHINE-APPLIQUE,
EMBROIDERY, MACHINE-QUILTING

My quilt is a representation of the atomic testing carried out by the British Government in the Australian desert at Maralinga: the 'Black Mist' disaster. The hot colours of the fireball signify the force of the bomb and also the turmoil felt by the Aborigines as they endured sickness, death and relocation because of the poisoned air and land. The peaceful area, depicting new growth and sunshine, is a sign of hope with the news that the British Government has agreed to contribute nearly half of the cost of decontaminating the radioactive waste left at Maralinga.

I have recorded on the quilt what the uninformed Aboriginal people saw and their confusion at the time of the bombing.

HELEN BROOK

Pine Point, South Australia

I WAS THINKING IT MIGHT BE A DUST STORM
MATERIALS: HAND-DYED COTTON
TECHNIQUES: MACHINE-PIECING,
MACHINE-QUILTING,
MACHINE-EMBROIDERY

January 1994 and the raging fires around Sydney brought back memories of Ash Wednesday and the fires in South Australia eleven years ago. My family were involved in fighting fires in Mount Gambier and I remember the colours of destruction so well, and the blackened landscape after the fire.

One of my favourite techniques since moving from traditional designs to creating original work is the tuck, learnt from Caryl Bryer Fallert while I was touring the United States. This quilt, using the tuck and painted fabric, reflects my memories of the power and the fury of the fire, and the colours that filled the landscape as it destroyed everything in its path.

JAN TREGOWETH
Mount Gambier, South Australia

FOREST FURY
MATERIALS: COTTON, VILENE, WOOL BATTING, ACRYLIC PAINT
TECHNIQUES: STRIP-PIECING, TUCKING, TYING, MACHINE-QUILTING, PAINTING

A piece of Australian toile, some fabric with sailing ships on it, and a cotton printed with a rock pattern were the basis for my 'Sydney' fabric collection. Although not my usual pattern for collecting fabrics, these pieces seem to reflect so many of my memories after a visit to Sydney in 1993.

My ideas tumbled together as I began to construct the quilt. Representing the past, Captain Arthur Phillip is central to the design and is surrounded by the impossible triangle which represents Captain James Cook's extraordinary feats of navigation. City buildings, roads and parks represent the present. With so much of the future unpredictable and change happening so fast, I have used the gold surround as the future, peeling back each day to become the present, bright with possibilities.

SANDRA BURCHILL
Malanda, Queensland

FROM TODAY
MATERIALS: AUSTRALIAN TOILE, COTTON, LUREX
TECHNIQUES: MACHINE-PIECING, MACHINE-APPLIQUE,
HAND-APPLIQUE, HAND-QUILTING

COUNTRY COLOURS
MATERIALS: COTTON, POLYCOTTON,
DYED AND BLEACHED FABRICS
TECHNIQUES: HAND-PIECING,
APPLIQUE, EMBROIDERY,
HAND-QUILTING

My home in central Victoria is surrounded by tall gums and lovely golden wattle with many varieties of birds and Australian fauna nearby.

This quilt expresses my love of the country, the beauty of everything Australian. From a small sketch, I gradually built my quilt, using an overdyed fabric for the tree and adding extra branches where necessary. I enlarged or reduced pictures of the animals as necessary, mostly without the aid of a photocopier. Uluru, an essential part of any Australian landscape is central to the design, highlighting the ancient land and providing a spiritual focus.

MERLE THATCHER

Maryborough, Victoria

Humour has been a popular form of political commentary in Australia since the early 1830s, allowing us to comment on our political system without necessarily making the audience laugh. Living in Canberra, it is impossible to avoid politics.

With all circus performances banned by our local government, my quilt suggests that, even though the real circus may no longer perform in Canberra, our political circus continues to be a showcase of entertainment for the whole nation — regardless of one's political persuasion.

KERRILYN GAVIN

Chapman, Australian Capital Territory

UNDER THE BIG TOP
MATERIAL: COTTON
TECHNIQUES: MACHINE-PIECING,
MACHINE-APPLIQUE, HAND-APPLIQUE,
MACHINE-QUILTING

The effect of human intervention on the landscape interests me. The bright colours and graphic patterning of the paraphernalia associated with the road and sewerage works in my suburb offer a continuing source of inspiration. Although ubiquitous, the barricades, plastic wrappings and painted symbols on the roadway are, by their very nature, a kinetic form of art; constant yet transitory.

This quilt is the fourth in a series based on the theme 'Urban Landscape', which I hope to explore further.

JUDY HOOWORTH

Terrey Hills, New South Wales

URBAN LANDSCAPE
MATERIALS: COTTON, PELLON BATTING (DOUBLED)
TECHNIQUES: MACHINE-PIECING, MACHINE-APPLIQUE,
APPLIED CRAYONS, HAND-QUILTING, MACHINE-QUILTING

As I look into the landscapes that surround me, I am drawn to interpret them in fabric; to dye and print, so that the spectrum of colours I have to work with comes closer to what I see in nature. The colours deep within the Dandenong Ranges in Victoria where I live are not the greens of first glance, but a myriad of greens, oranges, pinks and browns.

Inspired by these colours, I am compelled to move away from my love of the life-ordering quality of the traditional quilt, and to paint and draw with fabric to capture the magic.

JOY SERWYLO
Upwey, Victoria

FOREST III
MATERIALS: COTTON, POLYCOTTON,
HAND-DYED AND PRINTED COTTON
TECHNIQUES: COLLAGE SECURED
BY FREE MACHINE-QUILTING

KEEP THE ASPIDISTRA FLYING
MATERIALS: COTTON, PERMANENT
TEXTILE INK, CROCHET COTTON
TECHNIQUES: AIRBRUSHING,
HAND-QUILTING

When I think of Australia's history, I think not only of our Aboriginal heritage and the Aboriginal connection with the earth and sky, but also of our English connections. Potted aspidistras are very English and always make me think of Victorian drawing rooms.

I have combined these thoughts in executing this work, using airbrushing and bold black quilting with crochet cotton to enhance the design.

NOLA GIBSON
Narre Warren, Victoria

Due to my fine arts background, I have always used my artisitic techniques as a means of expressing an idea. In this piece, I began with multicoloured curtain fabrics to use as a base for printing to develop images of bush textures. With overprinting, I subdivided the original pattern, turning the separate pieces into a cohesive, multitextured whole.

To achieve the impression of the changing colours of the Australian bush, I have constructed the quilt using crazy strip-piecing. This is a technique that has evolved over the last few years as I developed my forest series.

WENDY LUGG

Bull Creek, Western Australia

BUSH TEXTURES
MATERIALS: COTTON, POLYESTER, FABRIC-PRINTING INK
TECHNIQUES: MACHINE-PIECING, MACHINE-QUILTING, HAND-PRINTING

I am fortunate to live in a national park, so I am surrounded by a marvellous canopy, amazing rock formations and exquisite ground coverings of flowers and grasses — especially my favourite, 'Grandfather's beard', which I have stylised in this work.

This quilt evokes the colours of my particular environment: the vast blue sky; blue-green mountains; grey rocks and soft pink sandstones; and, of course, the huge variety of tiny flowers which hide under the greenery down on the ground.

DIANNE JONES
Wentworth Falls, New South Wales

UP ... DOWN ... ALL AROUND
MATERIALS: HAND-DYED AND PAINTED COTTON, SILK, CORDUROY
TECHNIQUES: APPLIQUE, MACHINE-PIECING, MACHINE-EMBROIDERY, MACHINE-QUILTING

Whatever the disaster, man-made or natural, I am always impressed by the availability of volunteers to 'help a mate' in the true Aussie spirit.

My quilt pays tribute to all these volunteers: the women from a Sydney four-wheel drive club who took food to the drought-stricken farmers, all the ordinary people who rallied to help the flood victims at Nyngan, and the Bush Fire Brigades and volunteers during the 1994 Sydney bushfires. The green depicts the wind and cyclone disasters, with the helping hands there to assist. With so much of our leisure time focussed on the sea, I have dedicated the bottom panel to our lifesavers and marine rescue service. The top panel represents Uluru, Australia's spiritual heart.

DALE BROWN
Nowra, New South Wales

A LAND OF VOLUNTEERS – TRUE OZ SPIRIT
MATERIALS: COTTON, POLYCOTTON, STARS, BEADS
TECHNIQUES: STRIP-PIECING, REVERSE-APPLIQUE, APPLIQUE

My quilt celebrates a narrow escape from a bushfire twenty-five years ago. My clothes were scorched by red-hot gum leaves carried along by the gale force wind. I wanted to create the atmosphere of flames racing through the grass and up the trees, with masses of hot debris flying through the air.

The beginning of the fire is captured in the strong red border, with the inner panel representing the ash and embers after the fire has passed.

BARBARA MACEY
Mount Waverley, Victoria

FLAMES, ASH, EMBERS
MATERIALS: COTTON, SYNTHETIC,
HAND-PRINTED FABRIC, PELLON BATTING
TECHNIQUES: PRESSED PIECING,
MACHINE-QUILTING, FABRIC PRINTING

I made this quilt after a very enjoyable trip to north-western Western Australia, travelling by road through the Kimberleys and the Bungle Bungles to the west coast, Broome and Coral Bay.

The quilt shows the red earth, the stripes of the Bungle Bungles, palm trees clinging to the tops of red rocks, and the gorges and creeks formed by the torrential rain in the wet. The beautiful west coast, with its fish, turquoise sea and red earth is captured on the left side of the quilt.

ANNETTE CLAXTON

Kent, England

NWWA (NORTH-WEST WESTERN AUSTRALIA)
MATERIALS: COTTON, POLYESTER BATTING
TECHNIQUES: MACHINE-PIECING, MACHINE-QUILTING

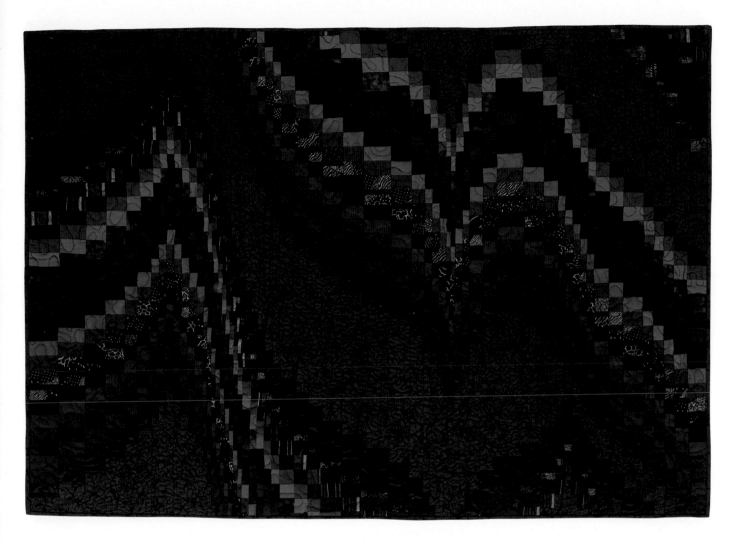

QUEENSLAND'S BLUE LIGHTNING
MATERIALS: COTTON, POLYESTER,
SATIN, POLYESTER BATTING
TECHNIQUES: MACHINE-PIECING,
MACHINE-QUILTING

I am fascinated by the colours in the boulder opals found in Queensland. These poor cousins of the more popular opal reveal a brilliant blue, contrasting with a subdued brown from the surrounding rock.

I was inspired to capture these jewel-like colours and contrasts, overdyeing olive fabrics to achieve just the right shade of brown. The opals are always fragmented, causing an interplay of light and shadow. To interrupt the rectangular shapes of the Bargello stripping and reflect this fragmentation, I used two different sizes of stipple-quilting and rearranged and superimposed bands when piecing.

LARRAINE SCOULER

Glenbrook, New South Wales

While eating breakfast each morning, I am surrounded by a cacophony of noise and a riot of colour as the rainbow lorikeets, and eastern and paleface rosellas join me. Fighting for a space on the feeders, they jostle and argue with each other in a dazzling whirl of colour in the leaves.

I wanted to capture this sensory delight in my quilt, using the black background to highlight my palette of colour, allowing myself the freedom to use the fabric without the constraints of a pattern.

WENDELEE WEIS
Worongary, Queensland

**PARROTS IN THE TREES –
COLOUR AND MOVEMENT**
MATERIALS: VELVET, DUPION SILK,
SATIN, SILK THREAD
TECHNIQUES: RUCHING, PIECEWORK,
APPLIQUE, HAND-QUILTING

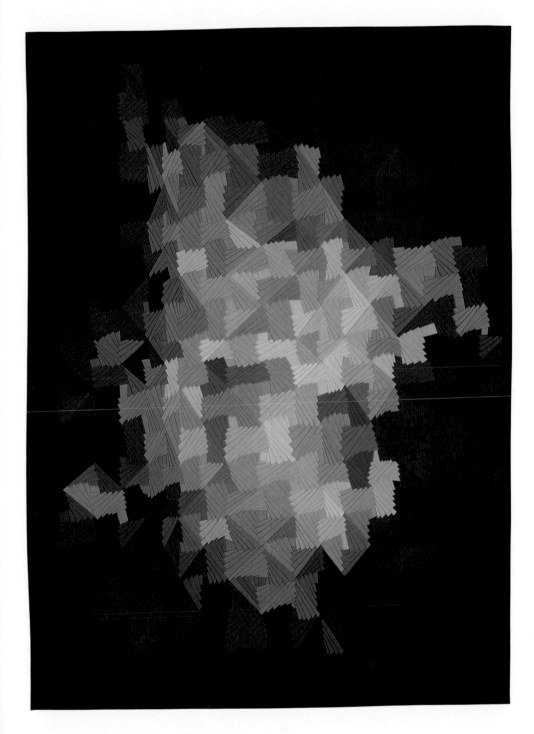

My starting point in this quilt is yellow, the colour of the desert. It provides the contrast for all the other colours, brightening and highlighting as it interacts with the greens and blues of the fertile areas and the blue of the ocean. Hints of red move through the colours, suggesting heat. Working on a distorted log cabin foundation grid, with no two blocks the same, I have tried to capture the colours around me, and the colours in my imagination, as if viewed from a distance.

KERRY GADD

Wodonga, Victoria

FROM A DISTANCE
MATERIALS: COTTON, PELLON BATTING
TECHNIQUES: MACHINE-PIECING ONTO
A FOUNDATION, TYING

Sailing the Whitsunday Passage in 1993, I found the tranquillity of the waters reflected in my thoughts: I felt an overwhelming peace that is not easily obtained in busy city life. The Barrier Reef was fascinating, and the isolation on board provided a revitalisation of mind and body. My quilt is a collection of my thoughts: the beauty of the waters contrasting with the earth and the forbidding yet alluring outback. The colours of earth and water are combined with quilting stitched to echo an Aboriginal design.

ANNA BROWN

Frenchs Forest, New South Wales

ORIGINS
MATERIALS: SILK, POLYESTER, COTTON
TECHNIQUES: MACHINE-PIECING, HAND-QUILTING

RED ROCK – ULURU
MATERIALS: SILK, HAND-PRINTED
FABRIC FROM THE TIWI TRIBE,
ANTIQUE BEADS, BROCADES, CHIFFON
TECHNIQUES: STRIP-PIECING,
FREE MACHINE-EMBROIDERY,
MACHINE-QUILTING, LAYERING,
COLLAGE

The impact of Uluru, right in the centre of the continent, surrounded by vast deserts and an endless sky, left a lasting impression on me.

The red rock dominates my quilt, reflecting my view that this landmark must be preserved and protected for future generations.

Shimmering images are part of the desert landscape. I have painted with threads, using gold, silks and satins to bring out the richness of the changing colours I observed while climbing Ayers Rock.

SUE WADEMAN
Springwood, New South Wales

EIW 448 is the number plate of our four-wheel drive vehicle. It takes us to remote places throughout the outback and allows us to enjoy their grandeur and beauty.

Since 1942, when I received a copy of The Way of the Whirlwind by Mary and Elizabeth Durack, I have enjoyed the images of the outback, their vibrant, rich colours and the myths that surround them. As we travel, the desert stretches are long and dusty. The gorges, with their water holes and vegetation, provide a stark contrast, not only in structure but in the deepness of the colours. I love to dive into the water holes, to be completely submerged and to become part of the image.

My quilt emerges as I work, without a plan, reflecting my emotions and my innermost feeling as I react to the environment and my memories.

JENNIFER LEWIS

Balnarring Beach, Victoria

EIW 448
MATERIALS: COTTON, POLYCOTTON
TECHNIQUES: HAND-APPLIQUE,
MACHINE-APPLIQUE,
HAND-PIECING, EMBROIDERY

RED EARTH, BLUE SKY AND SUN
MATERIALS: COTTON, COTTON BLEND
TECHNIQUES: FREE-MOTION MACHINE-QUILTING

A visitor to Australia, flying over Darwin for the first time, sees vast expanses of red-brown earth and the blue, blue sky. Warmed by the sun and bathed in its light, these images form lasting impressions, which I have captured in my quilt.

ROSLYN MOULES
Bonnet Bay, New South Wales

Outside my window is a beauti-ful tree. As the golden sunlight shines through its leaves, the tree echoes the colours of the nearby bushland.

To capture the great variety of greens and golds I discovered as I studied my tree, I used over one hundred and fifty fabrics in the four hundred and fifty appliquéd leaves. My passion is for tradi-tional designs and this work replicates one of my favourite designs from the 1890s, called 'Autumn Leaf', but uses the Australian bushland colours.

JUDY DAY

Lindfield, New South Wales

JUST LEAVES
MATERIALS: COTTON, POLYESTER BATTING
TECHNIQUES: HAND-APPLIQUE, HAND-PIECING,
BORDERS ALSO PIECED BY HAND

COLOURS OF AUSTRALIA   64

The combination of blue and gold in familiar landscapes has for a long time been overlooked as being very Australian. Blue sea, blue sky, golden sands and dunes, golden dry grass in our white summer light, even the soft blues and golds in the bush provide this wonderful combination of colour. When I came over the marram grass dune one spring morning, I was 'knocked out' by the blue ocean and rolling surf. This quilt captures the image, with the movement of the waves achieved with dyeing and the overlay of the quilting stitch. The grass movement was achieved by photocopying marram grass and then overprinting different groups of grasses onto the fabric.

BRONWEN GIBBS
Somers, Victoria

HIDDEN LANDSCAPES
MATERIALS: HAND-PRINTED AND DYED COTTON, COTTON BATTING
TECHNIQUES: GOCCO PRINTING, MACHINE-PIECING, MACHINE-QUILTING

Politicians in Australia would love our country to be known for its vocation ethic, but I think we have a wonderful vacation ethic instead. Living on the 'verandah of the continent' (the coast) as most of us do, we enjoy the bright clear colours of summer and casual beach holidays.

My quilt captures the memories of many enchanted vacations spent by the sea enjoying the sun and celebrating life.

ALYSOUN RYVES
Woolwich, New South Wales

'To arrive where we started and know the place for the first time, I thought, as Sydney's golden beaches appeared strung out like a necklace around the grey-green city, dancing in the morning sunlight.' This quote from The Road from Coorain by Jill Ker Conway inspired me to capture the essence of Sydney in this quilt: the beaches, the city buildings and the vegetation.

I consider the design and layout of my quilt the most important part. As I attempted to 'let go all the rules', I found that the use of fraying fabrics allowed the quilt to keep developing over time and, with friction and tension, to change.

ALISON MUIR

Sydney, New South Wales

SYDNEY
MATERIALS: SILK, POLYCOTTON, COTTON
TECHNIQUES: MACHINE-APPLIQUE,
MACHINE-QUILTING

With a supply of flag bunting and an irrepressible sense of humour, I set about putting my thoughts about banana republics and changing flags together, sensing a need to 'run it up the flagpole and see who salutes'.

I wanted the quilt to be interesting, whether it was viewed from afar or given careful close scrutiny, so the stars of the Southern Cross are only seen at close range, while the banana remains the overriding feature, seen at any distance. References to the Koori flag can also be seen with the black, yellow and red borders. As the quilt evolved, many techniques were employed that were not necessarily planned, including French knots, painted and overdyed fabrics and coloured-in OZ fabric so that it reads NO, NO, NO.

JUDY MCDERMOTT
Thornleigh, New South Wales

... **AND SEE WHO SALUTES**
MATERIALS: COTTON, GOLD FABRIC, FLAG BUNTING, WOOL BATTING
TECHNIQUES: REVERSE-APPLIQUE, MACHINE-PIECING, DYEING, HAND-QUILTING, MACHINE-QUILTING, TYING

The colours that surrounded me in January 1994 were blacks and browns, greys and deep ochres. The dramatic changes wrought by the bushfires in the surrounding landscape inspired me to create a quilt that revealed a symbolic personal response, not a literal interpretation.

I used a limited palette of treasured Italian fabric samples, playing with subtleties of shade and tone. Tragically, the fire was not natural, not part of nature's cycle, and so I alluded to the Aboriginal need for connection to the great age of the earth with the traditional boulder shape, suggesting that we, too, should be carers of the land.

WENDY HOLLAND
Mount Wilson, New South Wales

EXPIRED PYRE
MATERIALS: SILK, SATIN, WOOL, COTTON, VELVET, MOTHER-OF-PEARL BUTTONS, FLANNELETTE BATTING
TECHNIQUES: STITCHING STRAIGHT ONTO BACKING THROUGH THE BATTING

For the Colours of Australia Exhibition I couldn't resist the opportunity to work on a project with local Aboriginal artists. Living on board the yacht Kelolo at anchor in Gove Harbour, north-east Arnhemland, I was ideally situated to undertake this project.

We built this quilt together, with Wuyuwa directing the painting and Catherine the quilting. The design speaks of the beauty of the sunset in the billabong, and the colours of the late afternoon when the Baru (crocodiles) are resting. The word 'Baru' comes from Wuyuwa's mother's dreaming and she has given special permission for its use. The Barramundi, silver bream and bony fish swim around the Baru.

CATHERINE BROWN, BARBARA PHILP, WUYUWA AND YANANYMUL MUNUNGGURR

North-east Arnhemland, Northern Territory

A grant from the Northern Territory Arts Council covered the artists' fees and material costs.

NORTH-EAST ARNHEMLAND BILLABONG
MATERIALS: COTTON, CANVAS, PERMASET FABRIC DYE
TECHNIQUES: ORIGINAL DESIGN, HAND-PAINTING, HAND-QUILTING

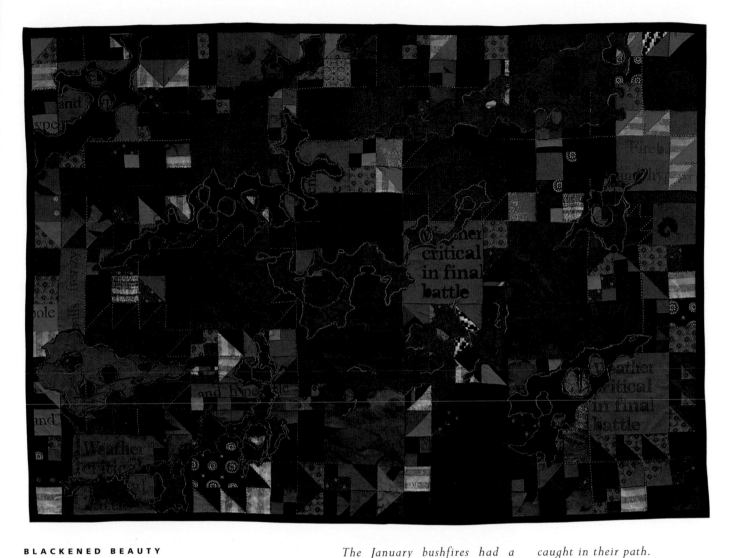

BLACKENED BEAUTY
MATERIALS: COTTON, ACETATE, POLYESTER, SILK, SCREEN-PRINTED COTTON
TECHNIQUES: MACHINE-PIECING, FREE-FORM MACHINE-APPLIQUE, MACHINE-EMBROIDERY, HAND-QUILTING

The January bushfires had a tremendous impact on people's lives: there were so many personal stories to tell. Yet the newspapers insisted on outdoing each other in sensational headlines, drawing attention away from the actual fires and the effect they were having on people caught in their path.

Using the 'Kansas Troubles' block with its swirling dynamic as the central motif, and some of my own screen-printed fabrics, the quilt develops these ideas and my reactions to such insensitivity.

LEONIE ANDREWS

Kambah, Australian Capital Territory

On ANZAC Day, Australians as a nation remember the soldiers of the Australian and New Zealand Army Corps who landed at Gallipoli in World War I and, through them, all the Australian soldiers who took part in all wars. Frank Rolfe, my husband's father, did return from World War I. I have embroidered his youthful face on a backdrop of rectangles, reminiscent of suiting sample quilts made in past times. The face is also symbolic of all those young men who went to war. The red poppies are for those sixty thousand soldiers who did not return.

My husband, Barry, wrote his father's story on the back of the quilt and sees the quilt as a tribute to his parents. Although not seen, the story of Frank Rolfe is an important part of my quilt — it must be there.

MARGARET ROLFE

Curtin, Australian Capital Territory

ANZAC
MATERIALS: WOOLLEN AND COTTON FABRICS, WOOL
TECHNIQUES: MACHINE-PIECING,
HAND-EMBROIDERING, MACHINE-QUILTING, TYING

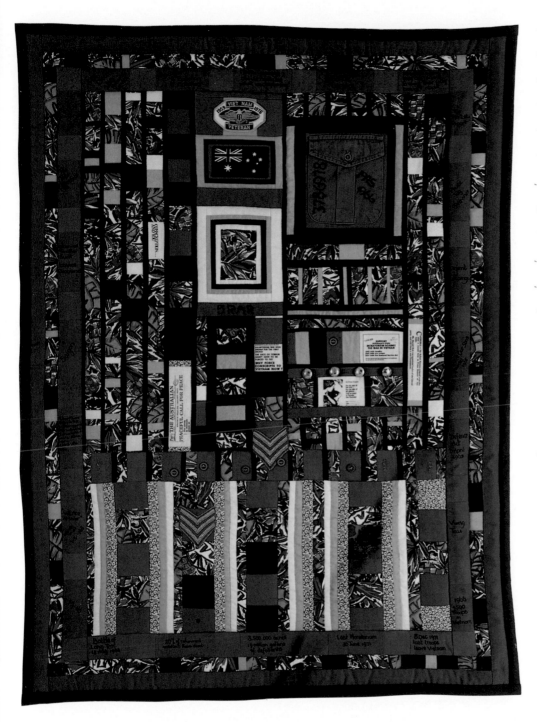

So many of my emotions are expressed in this, my first quilt. I was inspired to begin because of my deep feelings for those who served in Vietnam and the recognition of their plight as they fought for acceptance and a place in Australian history. Black is for the death in war, red for the horror of blood, yellow for the Vietnamese and army green for the men who served. I have tried to give the feeling of the jungle and army life, as well as make a statement about the Vietnam War and conscription.

LARAINE PICKETT

Carrara, Queensland

THE YEARS THAT WERE THAT SHOULD NEVER HAVE BEEN
MATERIALS: COTTON, PRINTED COTTON,
ARMY SHIRT AND BADGES
TECHNIQUES: MACHINE-PIECING, HAND-QUILTING

Australia is depicted as two women, one Aboriginal and one of European descent, dancing with their hands linked. They dance together but differently, revealing the variety their cultures bring to Australia as a whole. The skirts of the dancers form the map of Australia and the colours of the skirts extend right across the colour wheel, reminding us that Australia is a multicultural nation embracing all nationalities.

ADINA SULLIVAN
Grafton, New South Wales

TOGETHER IN HARMONY
MATERIALS: COTTON, COTTON/POLYESTER BATTING
TECHNIQUES: HAND-PIECING, HAND-APPLIQUE, MACHINE-APPLIQUE, MACHINE-QUILTING

'Crabs and Mangroves' is my gentle reminder of the importance of our littoral areas and the beauty we must all strive to preserve. The design for this quilt was first conceived in 1986 during a design class with Joan Schultz. Having discovered that I much preferred organic shapes to geometric ones, I enjoyed investigating this design, changing its orientation, size and interaction many times before actually committing it to fabric. The quilt was great fun to make. For the mangroves, I used fabrics I had dyed, and machine-embroidery to emphasise details. The work was assembled on a board, piece by piece. I made the dresses for the crabs first, but they were to be put on last, so I dressed the crabs each night, just for a touch of whimsy.

PAM WINSEN
Yeronga, Queensland

CRABS AND MANGROVES
MATERIALS: HAND-DYED COTTON, CHIFFON
TECHNIQUES: MACHINE-PIECING, RAW-EDGE
APPLIQUE, MACHINE-EMBROIDERY

QUILTS TO MAKE

Original designs from
Colours of Australia

MEASUREMENTS

Each quilt measures 90 cm x 125 cm (35½ in x 49¼ in). Sizes are adaptable.

SEAM ALLOWANCES

All the templates and layout diagrams in this section are given without seam allowances. This is to remove any uncertainty caused by metric or imperial measurements and the varying widths of presser feet of sewing machines.

For machine-piecing, the most common seam allowance used is 6 mm (¼ in). This is the distance from the needle to the edge of the presser foot on many sewing machines so, for an accurate seam allowance, run the edge of the fabric along the edge of the presser foot and the needle will be positioned exactly the right distance in from the fabric edge. On some modern machines the distance is 7.5 mm (⅜ in). If the needle cannot be moved from the centre to bring the measurement back to the standard 6 mm (¼ in), it may be easier to use the presser foot width as the seam allowance.

For fabrics that are prone to fraying, a wider seam allowance is suggested. For instance, the wool suiting used by Margaret Rolfe in 'ANZAC' (pages 72 and 82), could benefit from a wider seam allowance or overlocking by machine.

In general, the seam allowance for hand-appliqué is slightly under 6mm (¼ in). For machine-appliqué, there is no seam allowance unless the seam is first turned under, basted and attached with a blind hemming stitch.

TEMPLATES

MAKING TEMPLATES

To make templates, simply lay template plastic over the page, trace the shape with a fineline permanent marker pen, then cut it out. Remember, for hand-piecing the template does not include seam allowances.

For machine-piecing, the templates should include seam allowances. After tracing, add the seam allowance to all sides of the shape. Cut out this larger shape for the template.

Matching curved seams together is slightly harder than matching straight seams. To assist you, mark matching points along the length of both sides of the template, as pinning guides. This is particularly useful for piecing the background sections of Merle Thatcher's 'Country Colours' (page 87).

CUTTING

Fabric requirements have been calculated on fabric that is 115 cm (45 in) wide.

If the quilt is to be washed in the future, all fabrics should be washed and pressed before sewing. Remove all the selvages.

Position the templates so that at least one edge is on a straight grain of the fabric. Trace around the template on the wrong side of the fabric, then cut out, adding seam allowances, where necessary *(Figure 1)*.

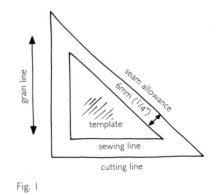

Fig. 1

Alternatively, a rotary cutter, gridded ruler and cutting mat can be used. With this method you can cut several layers together.

PIECING

HAND-PIECING

To align the sewing lines for hand-piecing, match and pin the corners of patches, starting at the ends *(Figure 2)*. For long seams, match seam lines, pinning them together several times along the length, matching all the corners *(Figure 3)*.

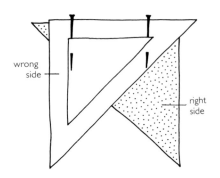

Fig. 2

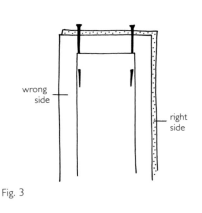

Fig. 3

Knot the thread and sew with a small running stitch from end corner to end corner *(Figure 4)*, leaving the seam allowances free. An occasional backstitch strengthens the sewing. Always end with a backstitch *(Figure 5)*.

Fig. 4

Fig. 5

MACHINE-PIECING

For machine-piecing, sew from raw edge to raw edge, through the seam allowance. No backstitching is necessary because the seams interlock at the beginning and the end. The width of the seam allowance must stay constant.

PRESSING

As each unit is sewn, press the seam allowances to one side, usually the darker side.

BORDERS

Border corners can be mitred or joint-butted like the Courthouse Steps pattern *(Figure 6)*.

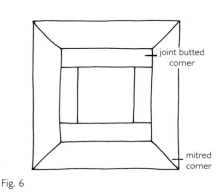

Fig. 6

A simple way of mitring corners is to cut the borders too long. Attach the side borders first, then, when you attach the top and bottom borders, do not sew through the seam allowance. Turn these ends back under until they make an angle of 45 degrees with the underlying border. Hand-appliqué the join and trim away the excess fabric.

Most of the border corners of quilts in this section are joint-butted. To make these corners, sew on the side borders first, then add the top and bottom borders.

APPLIQUE

There are several techniques for hand-appliqué. The one described here is the traditional way, but you can substitute your own favourite method.

1 Trace around the template on the right side of the fabric. Cut out the shape, adding about 5 mm (just under ¼ in) all around. Clip the seam allowance of any concave edges so they can turn under more easily *(Figure 7)*. Turn under and baste those edges that will show on top in the design *(Figure 8)*. To

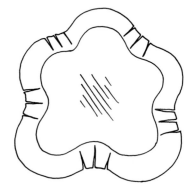

Fig. 7

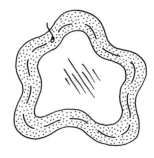

Fig. 8

create sharp points, turn under and baste the seam allowance on one side *(Figure 9)*; trim, then turn under the point *(Figure 10)*; finally, turn under and baste the other side *(Figure 11)*.

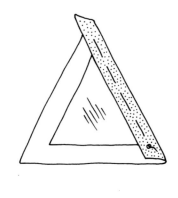

Fig. 9

Fig. 10

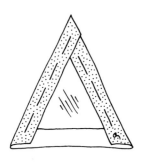

Fig. 11

2 Position all the patches, taking care to overlay them as the pattern requires. Baste the patches onto the background.

3 The stitch in hand-appliqué is just visible, so match the thread to the appliqué patch rather than to the background. Bring the thread up from the back so the knot is hidden and the thread emerges through the fold of the patch. Insert the needle in the background fabric just below where it emerged. Take it through to the back, then up through the fold of the patch again, about 1 mm ($\frac{1}{10}$ in) from the last stitch *(Figure 12)*. Secure with extra stitches any points and concave edges that have been clipped.

Fig. 12

4 To press, turn your work face down onto a folded towel placed on the ironing board. The towel will ensure that the appliqué does not flatten out too much.

The curved edge of small circles, like the wattle in Merle Thatcher's 'Country Colours' (pages 47 and 87), is hard to achieve. Make a cardboard template of the finished size of the circle. Cut out the fabric circle and baste around in the seam allowance, near the raw edge. Place the cardboard template on the back of the fabric and draw the thread tight over it. Press the piece for a perfect circle, then release the thread and remove the template.

STEMS AND NARROW APPLIQUE FRAMES

This technique applies where you wish to appliqué narrow strips of fabric, such as in the 'ANZAC' quilt on page 82.

Cut the fabric almost three times the finished width. Pin a needle or a pin on the ironing board so that the part showing on top is the desired width. Turn the seam allowances under and push the end of the fabric under the needle. Pull the piece through, pressing it as it emerges at the correct width *(Figure 13)*.

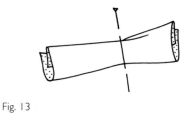

Fig. 13

REVERSE-APPLIQUE

Rather than stitch a shape down on top of a background fabric, the shape can be cut out of one layer of fabric to reveal the layer below as the shape. The footprints in the sand in Alysoun Ryves's 'Summertime' (page 84) are examples of this technique.

Draw the shapes onto the top layer of fabric, then baste the top and bottom layers together. Cut out the defined area, leaving a small seam allowance of about 5 mm (just under $\frac{1}{4}$ in). Clip into the valleys and concave curves inside this seam allowance *(Figure 14)*. Hand-appliqué,

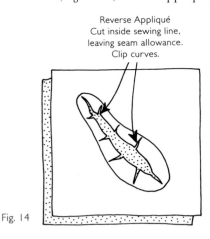

Reverse Appliqué
Cut inside sewing line, leaving seam allowance. Clip curves.

Fig. 14

using the needle-turn technique where the point of the needle is used to turn under a short length of seam allowance which is appliquéd, then turn under the next length. Continue until it is all appliquéd.

QUILTING

The five quilts in this section are all hand-quilted. Quilting takes up across the width and the length of the quilt, shrinking it. If there is a lot of quilting, as in Narelle Grieve's 'Toorallie in Bombala' (page 93), allow extra fabric if you want to retain the precise dimensions.

Use batting with a low to medium loft. Margaret Rolfe's wool quilt 'ANZAC' (page 82) is already quite thick, and uses flannelette instead of batting.

The thread used determines the look of the stitching. Most hand-quilters use traditional quilting thread, but Alysoun Ryves in her quilt 'Summertime' (page 84) has used DMC Perle Cotton and Margaret Rolfe has used even thicker wool in 'ANZAC' (page 82). The thicker thread shows up particularly well with the longer stitches, so that the quilting has an embroidered effect.

Most shapes are quilted along their edges (ditch-quilting), and large background areas are quilted down with filler patterns such as parallel lines and grids, or echo-quilted with evenly spaced lines parallel to the outlines of patches. Several filler patterns are used in 'Country Colours' (page 87) by Merle Thatcher, and Narelle Grieve used stipple-quilting to hold down

A detail from Wild Flower Study by Wendy Wycherley showing machine-quilting used as a drawing instrument from Quilt Australia '88

the background and make the main elements of the design stand out more clearly in her quilt, 'Toorallie in Bombala' (page 93).

TRANSFERRING THE QUILTING PATTERN

To transfer quilting designs, make stencils from the printed patterns and lightly trace around these on the quilt top, using a washable pen or pencil. A stencil in plastic, or even paper, is quite sufficient for a simple pattern.

If the pattern is repeated, first divide up the quilt into units to assist you. Do this by folding and lightly creasing or, with a very light touch, mark out the areas, using a lead pencil for light fabric and a silver or yellow one for dark fabric. Chalk is an alternative to pencil; it is easier to remove, but it could rub off before you want it to. For Narelle Grieve's wholecloth quilt (page 93), the sections are in rows. For Anna Brown's 'Origins' (page 91), divide the borders into squares, one for each spiral.

A more complex pattern can be handled by placing tulle (bridal net)

over the pattern and tracing over it with a soft lead pencil so that the marks are left on the tulle. Pin the tulle onto the quilt top and trace over these marks.

BASTING

To avoid the three layers of the quilt shifting and causing puckers, anchor them together with basting.

1 First, press the quilt top well and check the back for any loose threads or overhanging dark seams that could show through on the front.

2 Cut the backing about 5 cm (2 in) larger than the quilt top on all sides. Lay the backing face down on a rug or carpet and stab-pin it out, starting at the centre of opposite sides and working out to the corners, keeping the edges taut.

3 Place the batting on top and smooth it out. Centre the quilt top on top of the batting and stab-pin the edges into the carpet. (Alternatively, you can tape the layers to the floor.) Now that the three layers are held in tension there can be no puckers.

4 Thread-baste, using long needles and stitches. Make a radiating pattern, starting in the centre. Baste the quarter lines and diagonals, then fill in the extra 'rays' until the basting lines are no more than 15 cm (6 in) apart *(Figure 15)*. Fold over the excess backing to the front and baste this down to protect the batting from shredding during quilting.

For machine-quilting, pin-basting with safety pins is a quicker option *(Figure 16)*.

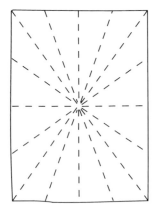

Fig. 15

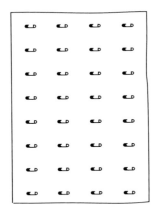

Fig. 16

HAND-QUILTING

Use a special quilting needle (the smaller the needle, the finer the work) and quilting thread (or a substitute if a different effect is required). Wear a thimble on the

Detail from Memory Piece by Rose Marie Szulc from Quilts Covering Australia showing unusual technique

middle finger of your sewing hand to push the needle through the quilt. Lightly stretch the quilt evenly in a hoop or a frame. Quilt from the centre of the work outwards, to eliminate the possibility of large puckers in the backing fabric.

Hand-quilting is made with a small, even running stitch. Begin with a controlled knot in the end of the thread *(Figure 17)*. Insert the needle about a needle length away from the quilting line, running it through the batting (not through to the back) and bring it up at the starting point. Tug on the thread so that the knot pops through the top layer into the batting.

Fig. 17

Make the stitches even and short. Insert the needle almost at right angles to the fabric surface, then lodge the eye end of the needle into an indentation in the thimble. Have a finger from the other hand pushing up on the backing fabric from underneath, and as soon as the needle touches this finger, push the needle back up to the surface.

Take just one stitch or rock the needle up and down through the layers to make several stitches. Pull the thread firmly.

To end off, make a backstitch, bringing a knot down to near the surface of the quilt and stab through the thread of the last stitch and the top and travel through the batting (do not go through the backing). Pull the needle up out of the batting about a needle length away. Tug on the thread to pop the knot down through the stitch and the top layer.

Crazy patch quilts, such as Australiana Victoriana by Wendy Saclier, do not usually require quilting

Detail from Impressions of an Australian Landscape by Jenny Martyn from Quilt Australia '88 featuring tying

TYING

Baste the layers of the quilt together then, starting from the back, pass the needle up to the front, then down again *(Figures 18 and 19)*. Repeat and tie the ends in a reef knot *(Figure 20)*. Cut the threads to 12 mm ($\frac{1}{2}$ in).

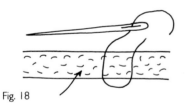

Fig. 18

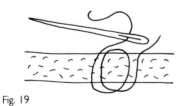

Fig. 19

Fig. 20

BINDING

SEPARATE BINDING

Four of the quilts in this section have a narrow, separate binding.

1 Trim the quilt back and batting level with the quilt front. The binding can be cut on the straight grain or on the bias. Cut the fabric 4 cm ($1\frac{1}{2}$ in) wide, that is four times the finished width. Fold the fabric in half, with the wrong sides together, and press. Press the seam allowances in towards the middle so that there are now three folds.

2 Open out the binding and, with the right sides together, align the edges of the binding and the quilt. Stitch along the closest fold line. Bind both sides of the quilt, then attach the top and bottom bindings, allowing extra length at both ends to turn a hem.

3 Turn the binding over to the back of the quilt and hand-appliqué (slipstitch) it down *(Figure 21)*.

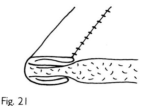

Fig. 21

SELF-BINDING

Merle Thatcher's quilt, 'Country Colours' (page 87) has a self-binding. The backing of the quilt is cut larger and folds over to the front (with seam allowances turned under) to form the outer green border. Fold over the sides first, then the top and bottom. Trim excess fabric at the corners, then fold them to make mitres. Hand-appliqué (slipstitch) the corners and the edges.

LABELLING

All these quilts are labelled on the back with the name of the quilt and the maker's name. They are variously handwritten, embroidered and machine-embroidered. Some have further information, such as the address and other details. Make your own label or sign in quilting so the quilt is identifiably yours.

A NOTE ON MEASUREMENTS

All figures are given in metric and imperial. Because they do not convert evenly, there is a slight adjustment to the conversions. It does not matter whether you choose to work in metric or imperial, but it is important that you stay with whichever one you choose and do not swap back and forth.

ANZAC

MARGARET ROLFE

LEVEL: BEGINNER

MATERIALS

Wool suiting, totalling 180 cm (70 in) in shades of brown, grey, navy and khaki, in light and dark tones, for the rectangles
30 cm (12 in) black cotton fabric for the frame
10 cm (4 in) red woollen fabric for the poppies
12 ply black wool
Chenille needle
135 cm (53 in) flannelette for the batting
135 cm (53 in) cream homespun for the backing
20 cm (8 in) grey woollen suiting for the binding
Tracing paper
Fineline permanent black marker pen

Before you begin, read the general instructions for quiltmaking beginning on page 76.

CUTTING

Cut the following pieces:
Rectangle A: eighty-eight in various colours of woollen suiting
Rectangle B: sixteen from the dark fabric
Frame (measurements include seam allowances): two lengths 5 cm x 112 cm (2 in x 44 in), two lengths 5 cm x 75 cm (2 in x 29½ in)
Poppy: three
Binding: 5 cm x 440 cm (2 in x 174 in) in total (with joins)

DESIGN

Rather than repeat the outline of Frank Rolfe, create the image of your choice. Photocopy a photograph of your chosen subject, enlarging it to the required size. Overlay the photocopy with tracing paper and draw in the most important lines with the marker pen.

SEWING

1 Lay out all the rectangles into a brick wall pattern of sixteen rows, arranging an interesting distribution of colours and concentrating lighter fabrics in a central oval. The top row (row X) and every second row start and end with a rectangle B and have five rectangles A. The alternating eight rows (rows Y) comprise six rectangles A.
2 Join the rectangles into rows, then join the rows together alternating the order of X and Y rows, to form the quilt top.

EMBROIDERY

1 Pin the tracing paper with the design lines over the quilt top and, using a long stitch length, machine-sew along the drawn lines as a guide for the embroidery.
2 Hand-embroider in stem stitch alongside the machine-stitching, using the black wool and the chenille needle. When the embroidery is completed, unpick the machine stitches, if they show.
3 Work the centres of the poppies in dense French knots, with long stitches radiating outwards.

APPLIQUE

Position the three poppies in the bottom right-hand corner of the quilt and hand-appliqué in place.

ASSEMBLING

1 Mark fine pencil lines as guides, then handwrite the legend of the quilt on the homespun back in the marker pen. Do not hesitate while writing or the ink will spread.
2 Unusually, the backing is added to the quilt at this stage so that when the frame is added it quilts the three layers together – the only quilting present. Assemble the quilt sandwich, then baste the three layers together.
3 For the black frame, press under 1 cm (⅜ in) hems on the ends of all

four strips. Prepare the frame as instructed on page 78. Position and pin the side strips in place, aligning the outside edge with the seam lines of the outermost row of rectangles, starting and ending one row in from the top and bottom edges. Use the photograph as a guide for placement. Increase the stitch length on your sewing machine slightly to accommodate the extra bulk. Machine-stitch down each edge. Repeat the same process for the top and bottom strips.

TO COMPLETE

1 Tie a knot at every corner intersection, starting the tie from the back so it is invisible from the front and the threads are exposed on the back. Cut the ends of the threads to 12 mm (½ in) long.

2 Trim the excess batting and backing, then bind the edges with a separate grey binding.

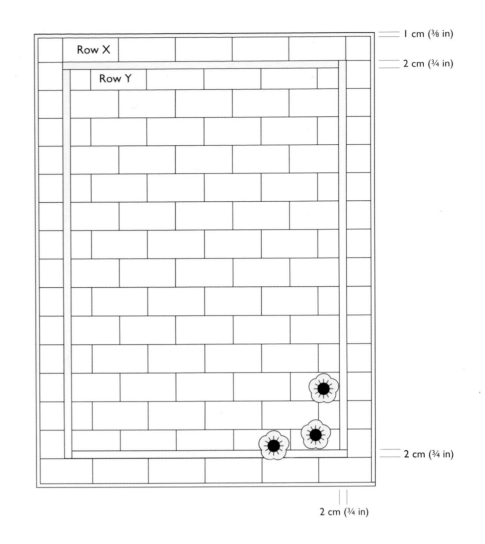

Row X

Row Y

1 cm (⅜ in)

2 cm (¾ in)

2 cm (¾ in)

2 cm (¾ in)

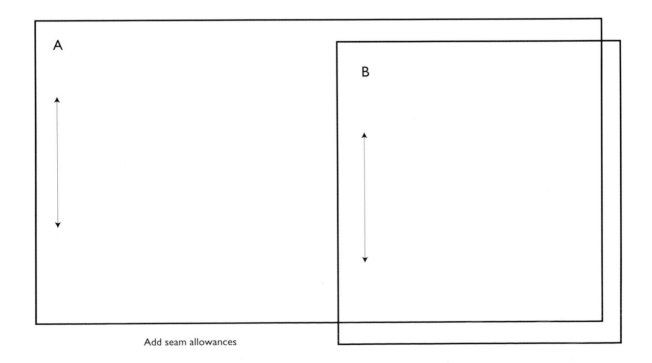

A

B

Add seam allowances

SUMMERTIME

ALYSOUN RYVES

LEVEL: INTERMEDIATE

MATERIALS

50 cm (20 in) of green ribbon

30 cm (12 in) each of red and purple ribbons

10 cm (4 in) each of two pale yellow fabrics

20 cm (8 in) of bright yellow fabric

10 cm (4 in) each of three blue fabrics

30 cm (12 in) each of red, green and navy fabrics

15 cm (6 in) each of fish print and hibiscus print fabrics

30 cm (12 in) of rainbow striped fabric

Scraps of fabric in ten colours of the rainbow

10 cm (4 in) of two striped fabrics

150 cm (60 in) of floral print fabric for the backing and binding

DMC Perle Cotton: yellow, green, blue, red, orange

Madeira metallic thread

Quilting threads in appropriate colours

Quilting needles

100 cm x 135 cm (40 in x 54 in) medium-loft batting

Before you begin, read the general instructions on quiltmaking beginning on page 76.

CUTTING

Cut the following pieces, using the photograph as a guide to the colour:
Triangle A: forty; Triangle B: twenty; Triangle C: thirty-four; Square D: seventeen; Triangle E, in floral: thirteen; Triangle E, in green: thirteen

Strips and borders: as indicated in the quilt diagram

Binding: 4.5 cm x 440 cm (1¾ in x 174 in) in total with joins

Make templates for all the appliqué pieces, then cut them out of fabric, adding seam allowances.

SEWING

CENTRAL PANEL

1 Strip-piece fabrics for the central panel, from dark blue sky to light sea, with a curved seam joining the land (see page 76 for tips on curved seams), then pale yellow to bright yellow sand.

2 Appliqué a verandah on one side, with the raw edge exposed at the bottom. Pull threads to give the fringed effect.

3 Appliqué a deck below the verandah, using ribbon for the railing.

4 Using the Perle Cotton, embroider the vines and the flowers.

5 Appliqué the sailboard, deck chair (with ribbon supports) and hat (using threads for the ribbons), a book on the sand, and the palm tree.

RED BORDER

Sew the bright red border to the four sides in any order.

SECOND AND THIRD BORDERS

1 Sew this border in the same way as the red border — in any order. Use the large hibiscus print on the sides, navy on the top and yellow on the bottom. Back the yellow section with orange fabric, then reverse-appliqué the feet (see page 78 for tips on reverse-appliqué).

2 Cut around some of the fish in the fish print fabric and hand-appliqué them over the adjacent borders. Make templates of the flowers in the floral fabric and cut them out of solid colour fabrics (or simply cut out whole flowers). Hand-appliqué the flowers in place. Embroider details on the flowers.

3 On the top night sky, appliqué three stars as shown.

4 Sew on a border of striped fabric in the same way.

NOTE: The fourth and fifth borders do not fit exactly; trim any excess length away after they have been attached.

FOURTH BORDER

1 Create two strips of flying geese design for the top and bottom borders by sewing two of Triangle A to Triangle B to form a rectangle *(Figure 1)*. Sew ten of these rectangles together to make the border piece.

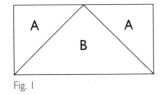
Fig. 1

2 Attach this border to the top of the quilt front. Trim the excess length. Repeat these steps for the bottom border.

3 The diamond border on the left side can be made piece by piece or sewn Seminole fashion. To sew the pieces together individually, sew Triangle C to Square D to Triangle C to make a parallelogram *(Figure 2)*. Join these units together in a row. Trim one end square and pin this end to the top left side of the quilt top. Sew the border in place, trim the excess length.

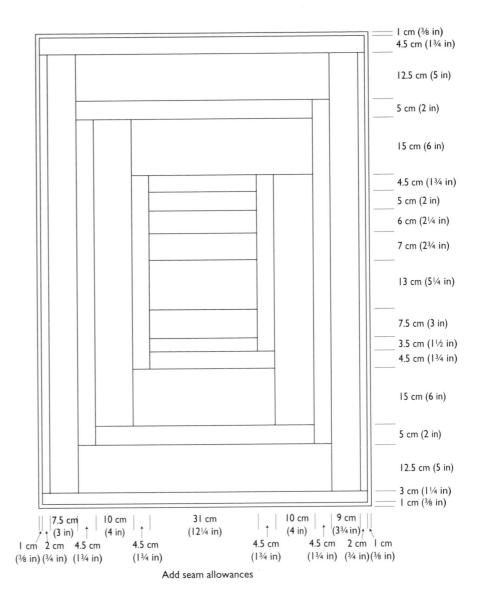

1 cm (⅜ in)	
4.5 cm (1¾ in)	
12.5 cm (5 in)	
5 cm (2 in)	
15 cm (6 in)	
4.5 cm (1¾ in)	
5 cm (2 in)	
6 cm (2¼ in)	
7 cm (2¾ in)	
13 cm (5¼ in)	
7.5 cm (3 in)	
3.5 cm (1½ in)	
4.5 cm (1¾ in)	
15 cm (6 in)	
5 cm (2 in)	
12.5 cm (5 in)	
3 cm (1¼ in)	
1 cm (⅜ in)	

7.5 cm (3 in)   10 cm (4 in)   31 cm (12¼ in)   10 cm (4 in)   9 cm (3¾ in)

1 cm (⅜ in)   2 cm (¾ in)   4.5 cm (1¾ in)   4.5 cm (1¾ in)   4.5 cm (1¾ in)   4.5 cm (1¾ in)   2 cm (¾ in)   1 cm (⅜ in)

Add seam allowances

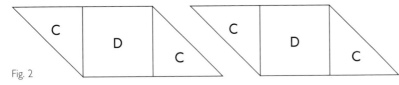
Fig. 2

4 For the triangle border on the right side, sew a row of Triangle E pieces together, attach the row to the right side of the quilt top, then trim the excess length at the ends.

FIFTH BORDER

On the left side of the quilt top, sew a narrow border of red. On the right side of the quilt top, sew a narrow border of green. Sew a border of striped fabric to the top and bottom. See the quilt diagram for the exact dimensions of these border pieces.

QUILTING AND BINDING

1 Cut the floral fabric to size for the backing. Assemble the quilt sandwich, then baste the three layers together securely.

2 Using long quilting stitches, quilt the word 'SUMMERTIME' along the top blue strip of the picture and the words '& the living is easy' in the sand.

3 Quilt wavy lines in the picture, radiating them out in straight lines through the rest of the quilt. Change the colour of the thread to match the predominant colour of the background.

4 Bind the quilt in the usual way.

VARIATIONS

In this medallion quilt, the central panel could be any scene and the colours and details would change accordingly. Clearly, reproducing this quilt precisely depends on the availability of a fish print fabric and a suitable hibiscus print fabric. If these are not available, substitute a bird print or even a jungle print. Be imaginative and explore all the design possibilities.

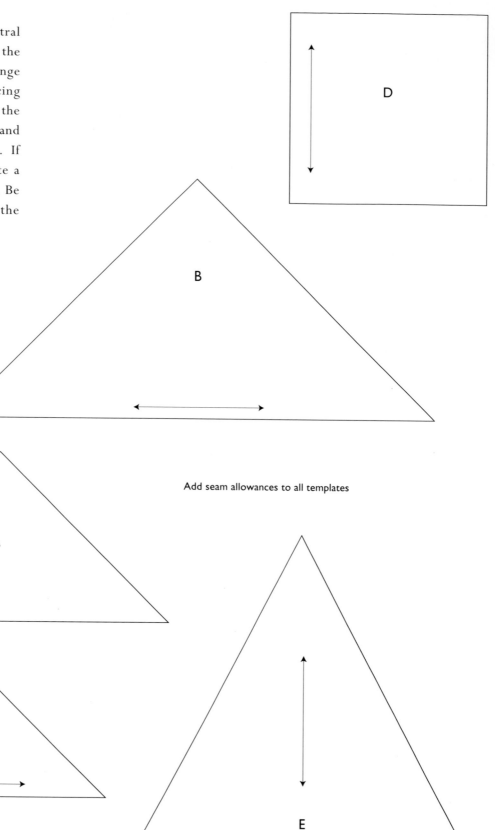

Add seam allowances to all templates

COUNTRY COLOURS

MERLE THATCHER

LEVEL: ADVANCED

The fabrics in this quilt include furnishing fabrics and textured fabrics which Merle has treated to achieve the effect she was seeking. For instance, the large tree is a piece of curtain fabric overdyed grey, while other greys and greens were also dyed to achieve the right colour. The sky blue is bleached back to create clouds.

MATERIALS

40 cm (16 in) each of blue and brown fabrics

10 cm (4 in) of white fabric

20 cm (8 in) each of assorted green fabrics

40 cm (16 in) of mottled grey/brown fabric for the desert

20 cm (8 in) of tan fabric

13 cm (5 in) of pale apricot fabric

10 cm (4 in) of orange fabric for the inset panel border

Scraps of a range of fabrics for the flowers, leaves, birds and animals

Embroidery threads in appropriate colours

110 cm x 145 cm (44 in x 57 in) of dark green fabric for the backing

100 cm x 135 cm (40 in x 53 in) of batting

Before you begin, read the general instructions for quiltmaking beginning on page 76.

CUTTING

1 Draw up the quilt from page 47.

The quilt diagram has a grid overlay to help you with the placement of the appliqué pieces. Draw a corresponding grid on your quilt drawing. Use either the grid or a photocopier to enlarge it to full size. This full-size pattern will be used for cutting out the background templates. For easy identification, number every shape on both copies of the pattern (reduced and full size) with corresponding numbers and an arrow to indicate the top.

2 Make templates for each background piece and mark the pinning guides on the long seam lines. Cut out the background pieces adding seam allowances.

3 Decide on your appliqué pieces. Some of them are illustrated here (some are full size while others have been reduced); for the others, you could use enlargements from books, magazines or from the quilt itself. Make templates for the appliqué pieces, then cut them out,

adding seam allowances.

4 Cut out the orange border of the inset panel.

SEWING

BACKGROUND

1 Using the photograph and the quilt drawing as a guide, piece the background, working from top to bottom.

2 Crease the background lightly into the same grid as in the quilt diagram. This will give you a guide for the placement of the appliqué.

3 Baste the appliqué pieces into position on the background, then hand-appliqué them. Embroider the details, such as the spines of the echidna; the feathers of the eagle, kookaburras and galahs; the veins of the leaves and the details of flowers.

INSET PANEL

1 Piece the background of the panel, then appliqué the features and finally embroider the details.

2 Add the border, mitring the corners, then position the completed inset panel onto the background and appliqué it in place.

BORDER AND BINDING

Trim the batting only to the size of the front. Fold the backing over to the front to form a 6.5 cm (2½ in) border all the way around. Hand-appliqué the border in place as a self-binding, mitring the corners.

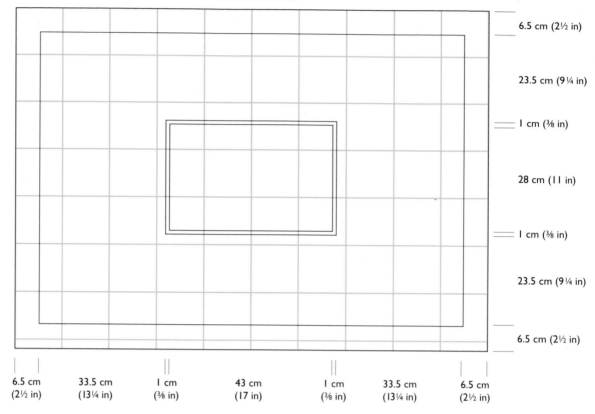

Add seam allowances

6.5 cm (2½ in)

23.5 cm (9¼ in)

1 cm (⅜ in)

28 cm (11 in)

1 cm (⅜ in)

23.5 cm (9¼ in)

6.5 cm (2½ in)

| 6.5 cm (2½ in) | 33.5 cm (13¼ in) | 1 cm (⅜ in) | 43 cm (17 in) | 1 cm (⅜ in) | 33.5 cm (13¼ in) | 6.5 cm (2½ in) |

QUILTING

Unusually, this quilt is bound before it is quilted because the binding forms the outer border and is itself quilted.

Outline-quilt all the shapes. Quilt down the large background areas with filler patterns: use parallel lines for the land, rippling lines for the water, diamonds for the land in the inset and radiating lines for the sky. Make a template of the border quilting pattern. Transfer it to the quilt and quilt the pattern.

VARIATIONS

Many of the features in this quilt could be incorporated into other designs. The inset could be eliminated, or enlarged to cover the entire surface.

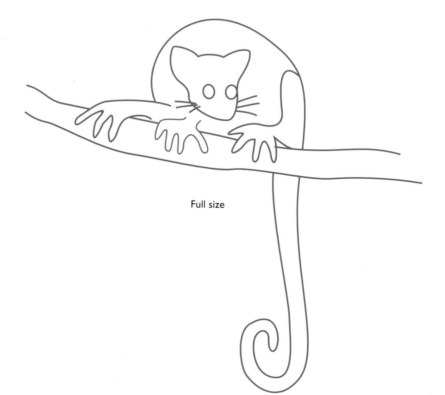

Full size

Half size

Half size

Full size

Full size

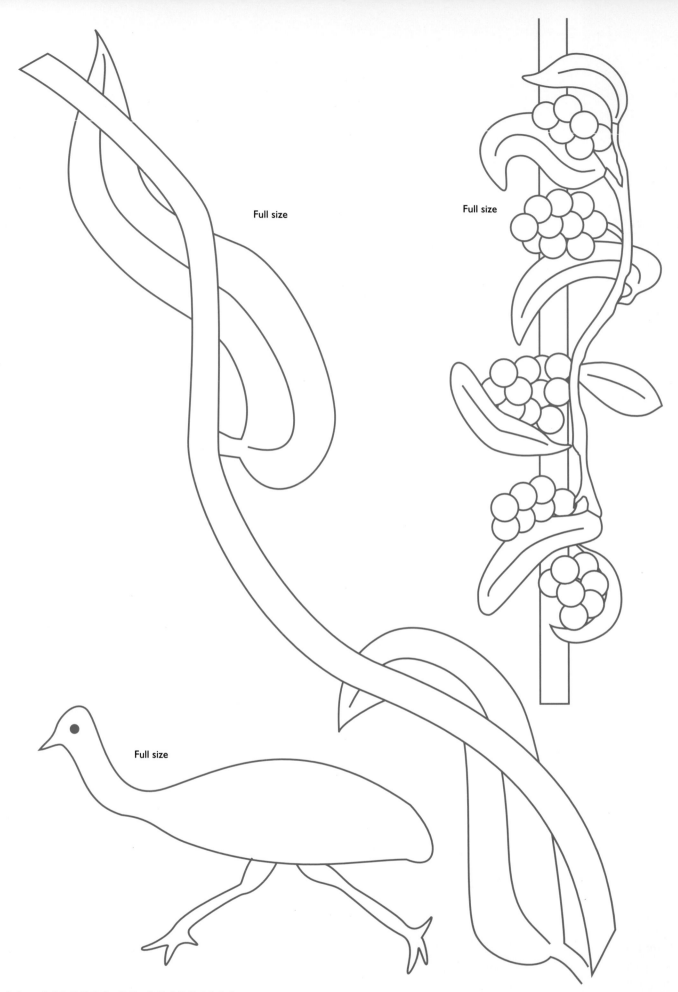

Full size

Full size

Full size

ORIGINS

ANNA BROWN

LEVEL: BEGINNER

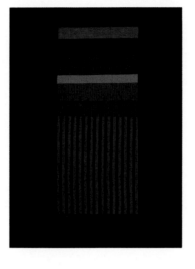

MATERIALS

10 cm (4 in) of blue cotton fabric

12 cm (5 in) each of turquoise, purple, orange, and tan cotton fabrics

8 cm (3 in) of yellow cotton fabric

50 cm (20 in) of brown-and-tan striped cotton fabric

100 cm (40 in) of black cotton fabric

100 cm x 135 cm (40 in x 53 in) of brown cotton fabric for the backing

20 cm (8 in) of black-and-brown print cotton fabric for the binding

Quilting threads, tan and black

Quilting needles

100 cm x 135 cm (40 in x 53 in) of medium-loft batting

Before you begin, read the general instructions for quiltmaking beginning on page 76.

CUTTING

Cut out the following pieces:
Refer to the quilt diagram for the dimensions of each piece. Cut out each one, adding seam allowances.
Binding: 4.5 cm x 440 cm (1¾ in x 174 in) in total with joins

SEWING

1 For the central panel, sew the colours together in the order shown: blue, turquoise, purple, yellow, orange, tan, brown-and-tan stripe.

2 For the border, attach the black side borders first, then the top and bottom borders.

QUILTING AND BINDING

1 Transfer the quilting patterns to the pieced top. Note that the quilting patterns have been reduced fifty per cent and must be enlarged.

2 Place the backing face down with the batting on top and the pieced quilt top on top of that. Baste the three layers of the quilt together.

3 Quilt the central panel with black quilting thread.

Add seam allowances

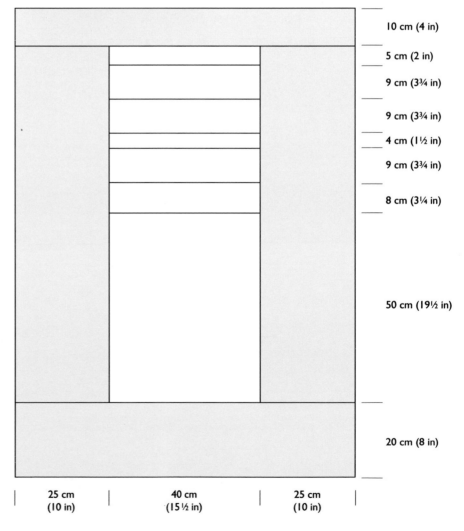

10 cm (4 in)

5 cm (2 in)

9 cm (3¾ in)

9 cm (3¾ in)

4 cm (1½ in)

9 cm (3¾ in)

8 cm (3¼ in)

50 cm (19½ in)

20 cm (8 in)

25 cm (10 in)   40 cm (15½ in)   25 cm (10 in)

4 Quilt the border with tan quilting thread, quilting the spirals first, then the filler of semi-regular parallel lines. The slight irregularity in these and the spirals allows them to be quilted with minimal markings.
5 Trim the batting and backing to the size of the quilt top. Bind the edges with the strip you have prepared. Bind the sides first, then the top and the bottom.

VARIATIONS

You can adapt this simple format to any size and colour combination. Expand the quilting pattern or substitute other symbols and features to complement your design.

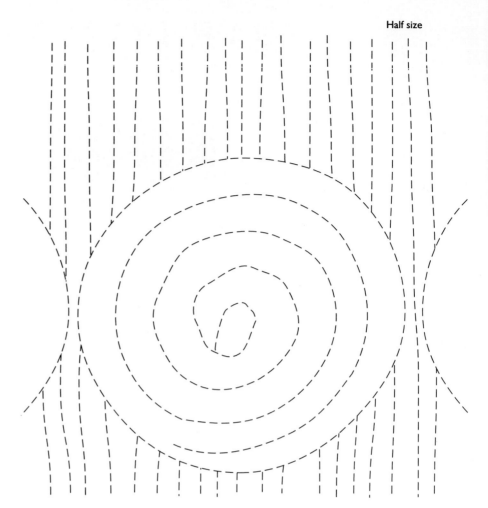

TOORALLIE IN BOMBALA

NARELLE GRIEVE

LEVEL: ADVANCED

MATERIALS

155 cm (60 in) cream synthetic
fabric for the top and binding
(cotton or sateen is also suitable)
100 cm x 135 cm (40 in x 53 in)
low-loft batting
140 cm (55 in) cream homespun
for the backing
Pencil and ruler
Quilting thread
Quilting needles

CUTTING

Cut the following pieces:
Top: 100 cm x 135 cm (40 in x 53 in) for the top
Binding: 4.5 cm x 440 cm (1¾ in x 174 in) in total (with joins)
Backing: 100 cm x 135 cm (40 in x 53 in)

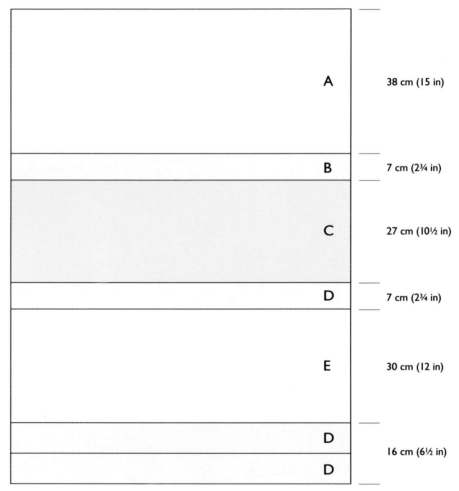

A	38 cm (15 in)
B	7 cm (2¾ in)
C	27 cm (10½ in)
D	7 cm (2¾ in)
E	30 cm (12 in)
D	16 cm (6½ in)
D	

Add seam allowances

Before you begin, read the general instructions for quiltmaking beginning on page 76.

QUILTING

1 Following the quilt diagram, mark the rows on the quilt top fabric. Transfer each quilting pattern into the appropriate row. Note that the quilting patterns have been reduced by fifty per cent and must be enlarged to full size.

2 Assemble the quilt sandwich, then baste the three layers together. Starting from the centre and working outwards, hand-quilt rows of straight lines. Hand-quilt the major features, then fill in background areas with stipple-quilting by subdividing a small area of the

Pattern A

Half size

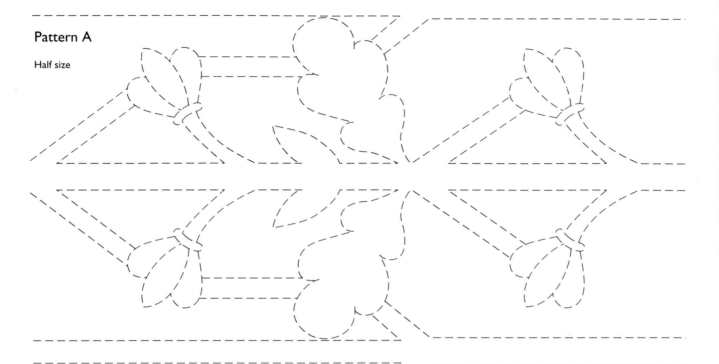

background into three or four irregular-sided shapes. Stipple the area in straight lines 1 mm ($\frac{1}{20}$ in) apart and parallel to one edge. Stitching in adjacent shapes should be in different directions.

BINDING

Trim the quilt, then bind it with the strips you have prepared.

VARIATIONS

To create your own design, (perhaps another pressed metal, plaster, or wrought iron design), photograph the subject on slide film. Project the developed slide onto a screen covered in white paper. Move the projector back from the screen until the image is the size required, then trace the lines of the image onto the paper. During this process, you can modify the design, adding to it or possibly eliminating some lines to simplify it.

Pattern C

Half size

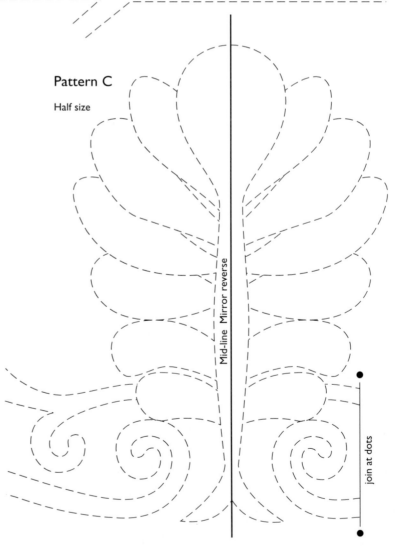

Mid-line Mirror reverse

join at dots

Pattern D Half size

Pattern B Half size

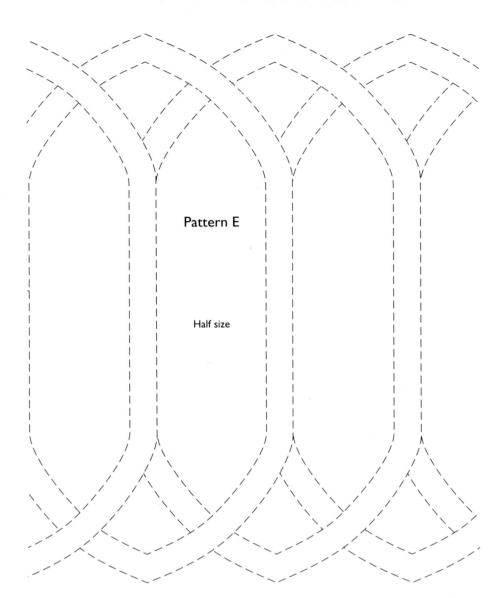

Pattern E

Half size

CONTACT ORGANISATIONS

The Quilters' Guild Inc.
PO Box 654
Neutral Bay Junction
NSW 2089

Victorian Quilters Inc.
PO Box 382
Myrtleford Vic. 3737

Queensland Quilters Inc.
GPO Box 2841
Brisbane Qld. 4001

**Quilters Guild of
South Australia Inc.**
PO Box 993
Kent Town SA 5067

**West Australian Quilters
Association Inc.**
PO Box 188
Subiaco WA 6008

Tasmanian Quilting Guild
C/- 2 Sherwood Close
Prospect Tas. 7250

Canberra Quilters Inc.
PO Box 29
Jamison Centre ACT 2614

**Darwin Patchwork &
Quilters Inc.**
PO Box 36945
Winnellie NT 0821